Appalachian Summer

Appalachian Summer

MARCIA BONTA

University of Pittsburgh Press

Published by the University of Pittsburgh Press, Pittsburgh, Pa. 15261

Copyright © 1999, University of Pittsburgh Press

All rights reserved

Manufactured in the United States of America

Printed on acid-free paper

10 9 8 7 6 5 4 3 2 1

LIBRARY OF CONGRESS CATALOGING-IN-PUBLICATION DATA

Bonta, Marcia, 1940–
    Appalachian summer / Marcia Bonta.
        p.   cm.
Includes bibliographical reference (p.   ) and index.
ISBN 0-8229-4095-7 (acid-free paper)
ISBN 0-8229-5693-4 (pbk. : acid-free paper)
1. Pennsylvania—Description and travel.   2. Appalachian Region—
Description and travel.   3. Natural history—Pennsylvania.
4. Natural history—Appalachian Region.   5. Bonta, Marcia, 1940–
—Diaries.   I. Title.
F155.B66 1999
917.4—dc21   98-40167
                                                        CIP

A CIP catalog record for this book is available from the British Library.

Portions of this book first appeared, in slightly different form, in the *Altoona
Mirror, Bird Watcher's Digest, Hawk Mountain News,* and *Pennsylvania Game
News,* as well as in *On Nature's Terms: Contemporary Voices,* ed. Thomas J. Lyon
and Peter Stine (College Station: Texas A & M University Press, 1992).

To Eva Luz Medina Bonta, our first grandchild, with love
and hope that you too will love the natural world.

EVA MANDALA

how curious
the thin stem of your larynx
resounding vigorously and true to every vibration

surprising
the crispness of your cauliflower lungs
that only yesterday lay nestled beneath
an arbor of maternal ribs

astonishing
the brightness of your chicory blossom eyes
newly opened along the side of the road
where all the world's refugees (five billion so far)
are raising dust

wondrous
the unknown mushroom of your brain
its natal ties to rocks and roots and burrows
developing (who knows how) such powers
to perplex enchant entrance or stun in rare
berserker rage

miraculous
all the branchings of your complex foliage
the whole forest trembles in your fingertips
reaching for the moon's resplendent breast
grasping at the sun's immanent nipple
with the kind of serene hunger that moves mountains
and makes the stoniest hearts spout fountains of praise.

DAVE BONTA
Daughters of Job: Songs for
a Revue of Female Masks

Contents

Introduction

WHENEVER HE COULD, my father headed us "up home" for weekends and vacations. Home was Pennsylvania where he had been raised, a poor boy of working-class parents, bright and determined to get a college education and make something of himself. He graduated from Penn State in 1936 with a degree in chemical engineering. It was not his true calling—landscape architecture was his true calling—but it was a way to earn a living in the depression years. Chemical engineers were being hired, although not in Pennsylvania. Only the string of oil refineries along the Delaware River on the New Jersey side needed engineers. And so my father crossed the river, and my mother followed. For forty years they were exiled from "home" to make a living and raise a family. But all the while they were exiled, my father told tales of his life as a boy in the woods of eastern Pennsylvania. I was the child who listened the hardest and who longed for the kind of free-ranging childhood my father had lived, roaming the hills and valleys near his hometown.

Even as a small child, the only time that counted for me was the time spent outdoors. We lived at what was then the edge of town near a chain of small lakes set amid a substantial woodlands laced with narrow trails. Being a girl, I was not allowed to go by myself into the wild area, but I usually managed to round up enough siblings and neighbors' children to accompany me. I was, in fact, a kind of female Pied Piper of the neighborhood who led the willing youngsters deeper and deeper into a maze of wooded wetlands and impenetrable thickets, cajoling the more timid ones through areas that might have appalled their parents had they known. Despite the sameness of the flat, southern New Jersey countryside, I had an unerring sense of direction in the woods that never failed me no matter how unfamiliar the terrain was.

Those explorations, though, were second-rate in comparison to our time in Pennsylvania. Pennsylvania had hills and even mountains, and I am a mountain person, preferring vertical rather than horizontal terrain. I also favor rushing streams over placid lakes and upland forests rather than lowland swamps. The southern New Jersey landscape has its own special beauty, but to me it remained an alien landscape. I passed my first eighteen years in suspended animation, waiting expectantly for my life to really begin. It would begin, I resolved, with college when I would leave New Jersey forever.

My first thought had been to attend Penn State, which is encircled by the ancient ridges of central Pennsylvania. Instead, I chose Bucknell University near the island-studded Susquehanna River because the campus looks westward over a verdant valley to a series of softly mounded green mountains to the west. I had no idea, nor did I particularly care, what courses the university offered. The view of the mountains was my sole criterion for choosing that university over the half-dozen other places I visited in Pennsylvania.

It turned out to be an excellent school for a budding naturalist, nurturing not only my Pennsylvania passion but my passion for learning as well. Time spent in stimulating classrooms was treasured almost as much as time spent roaming the nearby mountains and valleys. Again, because of my gender, I looked for suitable woodland companions. During my first two years, they were female friends. Then in my junior year I found my life partner, also the child of exiled Pennsylvanians, with the same feeling of "home" as I had.

First Bruce and I explored on foot—sometimes twenty miles at a time—and then on his motor scooter. Every suitable weekend we were out traveling the network of gravel roads built throughout Pennsylvania's forested lands. Returning late one evening, we saw our first aurora borealis display flickering across the splendid silence of the night sky. On another trip we stopped to walk in the woods and were caught between a pair of screaming bobcats. For an hour we sat in the underbrush and listened, hopeful, yet half-afraid that we might see them. Gradually the sounds faded away, and we were left alone, our minds firmly imprinted with an image of wildness in the midst of a peopled land.

During a hike in the Seven Mountains area, we encountered another symbol of wildness—a black bear—who turned tail and ran when we saw it, much to our relief. In those days we were uncertain about the intentions of what most people considered fierce and dangerous wild animals, novices, as we were, in the ways of nature. We had not yet seen many of the commonest birds, which is why I almost fell off the mountaintop at R. B. Winter State Park when I spotted my first scarlet tanager perched on a tree below the lookout. As I explained to Bruce, I had never quite believed that such a vibrantly hued bird lived part-time in temperate Pennsylvania, despite the assurances of my field guide. To this day no other birds, even those I have seen in the tropics, seem quite so beautiful as the scarlet-bodied, black-winged male scarlet tanagers.

By the time we graduated from college, we had covered a significant portion of central Pennsylvania on foot and on motor scooter, convinced of its inherent beauty and "homeness" to us. Someday, we dreamed, we would own a country place there. Sooner than most people, after our own few years of exile in Washington, D.C., we bought our first country home—in central Maine, however, not in Pennsylvania. And we had two sons with a third on the way.

Our five years in Maine were wonderful, but Maine remained alien to me. It was not "home." There were too many conifers and not enough hardwood trees. I noticed the lack particularly in the winter. The Maine woods are deep and silent, muffled in white snow and overhung by evergreen boughs, picture-postcard beautiful to be sure, but not home. Home woods are on-and-off white, continually freezing and thawing, brilliant with winter sunlight that pours down over the woods' floor, unimpeded by the naked silver and black limbs of hardwood trees. Such light and openness liberates my spirit. The Maine woods stifled me.

Only when we crossed into Connecticut, heading south at last into Pennsylvania, did the woods begin to resemble "home." Our Volkswagen van and U-haul truck were jammed with the accumulation of nearly eight years of marriage, along with our three sons, two of whom mourned the loss of the only home they knew. But we *were* going home, I told them, home to the mountains of central Pennsylvania and to Penn State where Bruce had a new job.

As we drove along, I sang out the names of the places we passed, weaving in tales of my childhood, my youth, our courtship, our collective memories of Pennsylvania. There, in northeastern Luzerne County, was where Daddy's people came from. The coal regions of Carbon County had nurtured my grandparents and my favorite great-aunt. That road led to Bucknell University where Daddy and Mommy had met. Just off Interstate 80, which had not existed during our college years, were the remains of the green wilderness we had explored as students. Our favorite place was Ricketts Glen State Park, with its twenty-eight waterfalls along an eight-mile trail and its tract of virgin hemlock forest, embodying the best of wild Pennsylvania. During our college days and our years of exile, we had returned to hike the trails in every season of the year, renewing, with each visit, our vow to return "home" as quickly as possible.

Deeper and deeper into the mountains we drove, sweeping past the largest road cut in the eastern United States. Except for one trip with the Bucknell University Choir, I was farther west in Pennsylvania than I had ever been before. So I had the sense of coming home and yet of entering new territory. That dual sense of familiarity and discovery has remained the dynamic that has nurtured me and will continue to nurture me for the rest of my life. Despite a fascination with the wider world beyond these ancient hills and valleys of an old, old land, a fascination we occasionally feed by traveling, no matter how far I go and how wonderful the places I visit, I soon find myself realizing, like Dorothy in the *Wizard of Oz*, that there's no place like home.

Having come home finally, at the age of twenty-nine, I was free to become what I had been working toward, through all my years of exile—a writer of place, eager to sing the praises of my own special niche on earth.

I had kept a nature journal spasmodically during our years in the city, recording only those parks and green spaces we fled to on the weekends. When we moved to Maine, my journal-keeping became more rigorous and was filled with the wonder and discovery of a novice to country living, parenthood, and the world of nature. I also read the old and new masters of nature writing—John Burroughs, Henry David Thoreau, John Muir, Hal Borland, Sally Carrighar, Ann Zwinger, and Rachel Carson, to name only a few—but I never considered entering the ranks of nature writers myself. Not, that is, until I came home. The incredible place we found for ourselves in Pennsylvania so overwhelmed me that I had to share my discoveries with others, just as Burroughs and Borland and Thoreau—all naturalists of place—had shared theirs.

We found our home on the Fourth of July. Following the vague directions of a local real estate dealer, we edged our bus along a narrow, gravel road that led up a wooded mountainside. Ferns and wildflowers covered the bank to our right while a small, rock-strewn stream tumbled below the road to our left. At last we emerged from the cool, summer-woods darkness into the sun-filled grounds and surrounding fields of what could only be described as a small estate with its two houses, a large barn, shed, springhouse, and garage, all possessing elegant lines and an air of faded grandeur. Well-loved in the past as the summer home of a wealthy family, its owners had sold it to less provident people, and already the decay had begun. But the price was right along with the mountain land accompanying it.

Perched near the top of the northwesternmost ridge in Pennsylvania's ridge-and-valley province, our home is accessible only by the gated, mile-and-a-half private dirt road we had followed. By western United States standards, the road is not particularly steep, nor is the mountain high (1,600 feet), but to most easterners, raised on roads paved to everywhere and used to convenience at all costs, our home is daunting to reach by vehicle and impossible on foot. We might as well live on an island in the middle of the sea.

Such a place has allowed me, as a woman, the kind of freedom from fear that remains an impossible dream for most women. In the early years, little boys clung to my hands or dogged my steps during most of my walks, but once the last son was off to school, I roamed alone and unafraid, an experience I had never had before. I was finally able to live, in my adult years, the kind of life my father had lived as a child. Our own land holdings now amount to 648 acres of mountain land, a veritable kingdom here in the crowded East, and our land is surrounded by other privately owned mountain land, most of which is posted against trespassers by its hunting landowners living in the farm valley below. Since they see me as unthreatening because my use of the land is nonconsumptive, the landowners have told me to ignore their signs. So, in essence, I have thousands of mountain acres to wander over and every season of the year in which to observe the life cycles of my fellow wild creatures.

This freedom to roam unafraid, gathering vignettes of natural happenings, harkens back to the sense of home our primitive forebears were thought to have had and makes me and my lifestyle a kind of throwback to a less complicated age.

Whether such a halcyon period ever existed is still debated by those who believe that humanity is naturally aggressive. Many feminist writers, however, postulate a time when females were dominant in communities as gatherers and nurturers, before the rise of male-dominated, violent societies. Whatever the truth may be about the ancient socializing tendencies of humanity, the sense of peace and fulfillment I feel, living here, is the kind of "home" spirit many females yearn for in these latter days of violence and hatred toward women.

Home should be a place of comfort, a womb in which we can float safely and warmly, buoyed by people we love and a landscape that nurtures our spirit. My childhood dreams of coming home to Pennsylvania have been fulfilled beyond my wildest expectations. As a female child I was infused with a love of the outdoors I could not fully indulge in because of both gender and place. As an adult I am home at last on land that will nourish me the rest of my life. And when my life is over, in final payment for the peace and beauty I have found here in harmony with nature and with humanity, my bones will in turn nourish the land so that my covenant with the natural world will not be broken.

I flip back through twenty-five years of nature journals and think of how much has changed and yet has remained the same, both in our lives and in the life of our Pennsylvania Appalachian mountain. Our three boys are grown now; Steve and Mark are married and only occasional visitors to the mountain. David has chosen to live and work in our guest house. This year our first grandchild, Eva Luz, born in Tegucigalpa, Honduras, on March 16, has come for her first visit. Now the pattern, begun so many years ago with our sons, of introducing them to the natural world as infants and carrying through, year after year, will continue into the next generation.

What Eva sees here is not quite the same mountain her father, Mark, saw when he arrived as an almost two-year-old. Then we owned 140 acres on top of the mountain; now we own 648 acres, including the entire watershed of the small stream that winds down through the hollow. Then, only the occasional bear wandered through every few years. Now bears are common here. Wild turkeys were rarely seen. So were porcupines. Both have increased tremendously. Cottontail rabbits and whippoorwills, the former ubiquitous, the latter breeding on the mountain, are now scarce. White-tailed deer and woodchucks have an overpopulation problem, and red and gray foxes are abundant. Eastern coyotes, not yet permanently in residence, have put in sporadic, fleeting appearances.

Bird numbers and species have also increased and diversified. Most neotropical migrants breed in our mature forest and over the last several years we have added yellow-breasted chats, Kentucky, cerulean, black-throated blue, and black-throated green warblers as breeding species, bringing our total breeding species to 71 and our number of species sighted to 163. Eastern bluebirds, once a rare treat to see, now not only breed here in both our nesting box and in hollow trees but frequently winter on the mountain as well. Red-bellied woodpeckers, infrequent visitors throughout the 1970s, are now permanent, year-round residents. House finches arrived here in the early eighties. They breed on the mountain and invade our feeders by the hundreds in early winter. Common ravens, once residents in this area, reappeared in the late seventies and are now seen and heard regularly all year long.

More and more wildflower species germinate every year. Two new orchid species—round-leaved orchid and nodding ladies' tresses—appeared in the early nineties at the Far Field. Wood betony sprouted on the road bank below our deceased neighbor, Margaret's, derelict house just two years ago. In the last two years fifteen new wildflower species have bloomed, and altogether we have found 192 species, 138 of which are na-

tives to our area. The others are alien species, most of which
were intentionally brought from Europe by early settlers as
useful herbs or favorite garden flowers.

We have more trails, courtesy of the logger who clear-cut
Margaret's land before we could buy it, and of David, who
has built several foot trails through the mature forest on the
Laurel Ridge side of the hollow. Once we owned the clear-cut
land we renamed the upper road "Greenbrier Trail" and the
lower road "Ten Springs Trail." On Laurel Ridge the Black
Gum Trail, following old deer trails, bisects the mountainside. Rhododendron Trail winds down into the lower end of
the hollow and Pit Mound Trail stretches from the stream up
to Lady Slipper Trail near the ridge top. Today we have over
ten miles of trails leading through a diversity of habitats—
meadows, mature oak/mountain laurel and wild black cherry
forests, a recent clear-cut, and a hollow with a mixed meso-
phytic forest (a diverse eastern forest type that develops on
moist but well-drained sites).

Despite what seems to be an increase in species diversity
and numbers, we worry about the long-term viability of both
natural and human life here. When we moved to the mountain, the four-lane bypass below Sapsucker Ridge had just
been built. Now it is connected to other highways and has
been upgraded to an interstate, so traffic streams past night
and day, traffic that we occasionally hear clearly if the air currents are right. We also suffer from noise pollution when the
air currents sweep up the hollow, bringing us the din from
what was once a small, family-owned limestone quarry in the
valley and is now owned by a huge corporation. The Sinking
Valley side remains peaceful, a farm valley with not even a
state highway running through it, now being farmed, in part,
by the Amish. So usually I can find silent places on the mountain where I can imagine that the late twentieth century's
technological excesses are a bad dream.

Eva, born into a noisy world, probably will not even notice

the occasional lapses. She will know only the world she is part of, a world with billions more people than the world I was born into, a world of vanishing forests and increasing desertification, a warmer world with more violent weather patterns, a world of diminishing fresh water and clean air, of species' extinction and chemical pollution, even in the far reaches of the Arctic and sub-Arctic wildernesses.

We have tried so hard to save a portion of the natural world for future generations, for our grandchildren. But for every step forward, it seems, we have fallen back even farther, beaten down by the rhetoric of politicians and talk-show hosts who refer to us as environmental extremists, responsible for all the economic woes of an overpopulated, overconsuming humanity.

Now that our grandchild is here, we can only say to her, "We have tried. Here, at least, is a piece of land still wild, still cherished, diminished by noise and air pollution and poor forestry practices, but not gone, a place where you, even as a female, can run safely and freely, as your father did, and experience what was once every human's heritage—a close connection to the natural world."

Eva came to us in mid-May and will stay through most of the summer, season of warmth and fruition, when the woods and fields are green and lush and overflow with singing birds, blossoming wildflowers, buzzing insects, and fluttering butterflies. In summer there are babies everywhere, wailing, peeping, crying for their parents, for food, for comfort, for the reassurance that their world will remain stable and safe and that they will mature in the goodness of time, each according to his or her own calendar. For the birds and deer, porcupines and woodchucks, it will happen in weeks or months; for Eva, the time line is more than two decades. All youngsters are part of the natural world, and their summers are halcyon days when life is young and stretches on forever.

*Appalachian
Summer*

Prologue

Not a perfect late May day—humid, cool, with rain clouds lurking on the horizon. But, no matter. It is Sunday, day of peace, and I am off into the woods to see what I can see.

I am a hunter without a gun or camera, a watcher of nature's creatures, hoarding memories of earthly treasures that neither moth nor rust corrupts. It doesn't take much to make my day—the sudden flaming of a bush turned scarlet by the setting sun, brief communion with a white-tailed deer who eyes me warily as I pass by, the organlike tones of a singing wood thrush. After years of going abroad every day, I don't expect nature to perform in the flesh as she does on television nature specials or to look as handsome and unreal as the photographs in nature magazines and coffee table books. For me, the experience of being out there in the flesh—seeing, touching, feeling, smelling, hearing—is all I ask.

Through sheer perseverance, day after week after month after year, I have my moments of beauty and wonder. Today I plan to walk Ten Springs Trail, but when I reach it, an inner voice urges me to climb higher, to take Greenbrier Trail. I surrender without a murmur of protest. Such urgings have

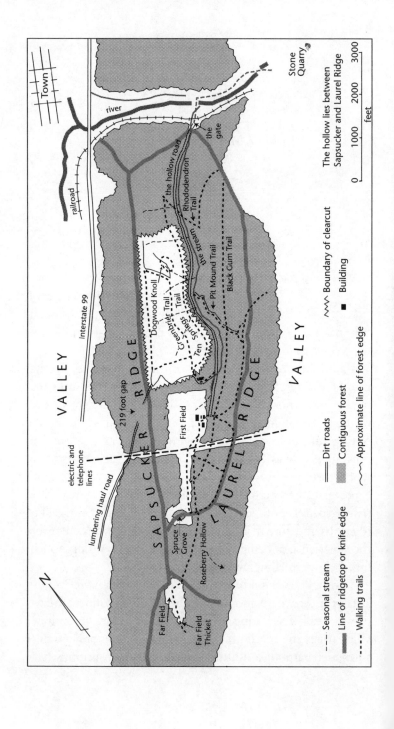

N

VALLEY

Town

railroad

river

Interstate 99

electric and
telephone
lines

lumbering haul road

SAPSUCKER RIDGE

219 foot gap

Spruce Grove

Roseberry Hollow

Far Field

Far Field Thicket

First Field

Dogwood Knoll

Greenbrier Trail

Ten Springs Trail

the hollow road

the stream

Rhododendron Trail

Pit Mound Trail

Black Gum Trail

the gate

Stone Quarry

LAUREL RIDGE

VALLEY

The hollow lies between
Sapsucker and Laurel Ridge

0   1000   2000   3000
feet

Dirt roads

Contiguous forest

Approximate line of forest edge

Seasonal stream

Line of ridgetop or knife edge

Walking trails

Boundary of clearcut

Building

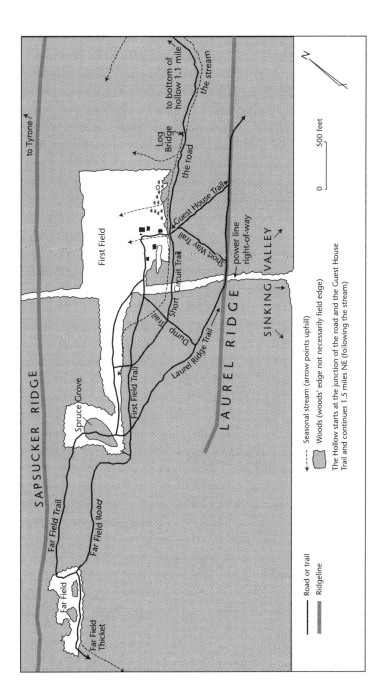

SAPSUCKER RIDGE

to Tyrone

First Field

Spruce Grove

Far Field Trail

Far Field Road

Far Field

Far Field Thicket

Log Bridge

to bottom of hollow 1.1 mile

the stream

the road

Guest House Trail

Short Way Trail

power line right-of-way

Short Circuit Trail

Dump Trail

First Field Trail

Laurel Ridge Trail

LAUREL RIDGE

SINKING VALLEY

N

0   500 feet

——— Road or trail

▬▬▬ Ridgeline

- - - - Seasonal stream (arrow points uphill)

▨ Woods (woods' edge not necessarily field edge)

The Hollow starts at the junction of the road and the Guest House Trail and continues 1.5 miles NE (following the stream) paid off before for me. After all, one path is just as good as another on the mountain.

Suddenly a ruffed grouse runs out from behind a fallen log, its ruff fluffed up, its tail spread, crying like an agitated mother. And so she is. Resisting the impulse to follow her enticing trail, I keep my attention centered on the spot where she first emerged and move slowly toward it. Ideal nesting habitat, I think, and, as if in answer to my musings, I hear a soft peeping.

Carefully I kneel in the mud and ask softly, "Where are you?" In an instant, tiny, light brown and yellow grouse chicks come running toward me, ignoring their circling, crying mother. They gather around my boots and climb over my extended hand. One even climbs up inside my pants leg, and I carefully extract it as it reaches my knee.

All the while I talk quietly to them in terms of endearment, admiring them extravagantly, a technique I have perfected to reassure fox kits and fawns. My voice seems to bewitch them, and I sit, as if in a charmed circle, while chicks continue to climb up my legs and into my lap. They are so tiny, so fast, that I fear I may trample one by mistake if I leave. I count them over and over again, and when I pick up several in an effort to keep all ten together, they do not peep in alarm. To my consternation I have become, in an instant, their mother, and, as such, an object of trust.

Their real mother hangs off in the background watching quietly. Afraid that I will upset the balance of nature if I don't leave immediately, I gather the downy chicks together, bid them farewell, and walk away. They run after me, peeping loudly. Having apparently arrived at just the time when the chicks were due to be imprinted on their mother, I am distressed to realize that they have begun to imprint on me instead.

"Stay there; stay there," I tell them, but still they follow on sturdy, determined legs. "Take care of your chicks," I tell their mother who has already metamorphosed from broody hen to protective parent. Then I run away at top speed, easily outdistancing them.

At last I look back. The mother has rounded up her little family. Reunited again, they have already forgotten the giant who had been briefly in their midst.

But I will not forget. I will tell the story over and over, like a mantra, to myself and others. The experience will remain as a shining talisman to illuminate the inevitable dark days of life. To have been mistaken for a ruffed grouse mother is a privilege few humans have experienced.

June

These are the days when skies put on
The old, old sophistries of June,—
A blue and gold mistake.

—Emily Dickinson

JUNE 1. Summer arrived on the mountain the day
we brought Eva home—May 19. It was over 90 degrees. Birds sang in a frenzy, the lilacs bloomed at last, and
the leaves of the black walnut trees finally started to open. A
tropical day to welcome our tropical grandchild to the temperate zone.

She adjusted quickly to her new home in the guest house,
sleeping eight to nine hours at night, nursing on demand,
and looking alertly around with her big blue eyes. Now she
smiles at us as she sits in her infant seat, and when Mark takes
her walking in her Snuggli, she sleeps contentedly. We imagine that a love of nature is already seeping in through her
pores. All of us are in love with her.

As I do almost every morning, I set out for my daily two-
hour walk shortly after breakfast. Today I followed the Black
Gum Trail. Its narrow footpath through our mature oak
woods tempts me more and more as I slip quietly along, lost
in an older, more pristine world, where nature, not humanity,

calls the shots. Surrounded by the chitter of chipmunks, enclosed in a wall of green, I listened to the calls and songs of eastern wood pewees and red-eyed vireos with occasional outcries from an Acadian flycatcher.

I found a long dead snag covered with *Polyporus sulphureus,* a deep orange bracket fungus edged in yellow, certainly the showiest of the genus. Altogether there were four large fungi, four medium-sized ones, and fourteen small ones that cascaded down the eastern side of the snag.

As I continued on my way I heard a worm-eating warbler and a great-crested flycatcher. The latter I consider the buffoon of the bird world because of its weird, incessant "wheep" calls that it reiterates ad nauseam through even the warmest part of the day. A troop of American goldfinches flew past calling, and a black-throated green warbler sang. Then I called in a black-throated blue warbler by pishing (pursing my lips and making a continual hissing sound) and watched it sing and forage in the trees. At the end of the trail, a wood thrush and ovenbird sang. June is indeed the month of bird song.

Next I headed up to the top of Laurel Ridge and back along the ridge top, taking a slight detour onto Lady Slipper Trail. As I descended the trail, a medium-sized black animal with a bushy tail suddenly jumped from a low tree limb and in a single leap was gone. Then there was silence and no movement in the underbrush that I could detect. It looked more like a fisher than any other creature I could think of, but this seemed impossible.

Most fishers disappeared from Pennsylvania because of both unregulated trapping for their luxuriant, dark brown fur and habitat loss when the forests were clear-cut and burned in the late nineteenth and early twentieth centuries. The last known Pennsylvania fisher was trapped in Holtwood, Lancaster County, in 1921, although according to William J. Hamilton Jr. and John O. Whitaker Jr. in *Mammals of the*

Eastern United States, Earl L. Poole found tracks of a fisher in the Blue Ridge Mountains in Berks County during the winter of 1931.

Fishers are the quintessential deep woods animals. They thrive in large expanses of mixed hardwood and conifer forests with a densely vegetated understory and plenty of fallen logs for cover. Like other members of the weasel family, they climb trees, prowling branches and the ground beneath for prey, as well as poking their heads into every available nook and cranny, looking for chipmunks, mice, shrews, voles, and squirrels. They are omnivores and also eat wild seeds and fruits and a small number of birds (mainly blue jays and ruffed grouse).

Fishers are most famous for their porcupine-killing prowess. Because they are quick on their feet, they attack porcupines head on, circling and lunging at the creatures and biting their faces until they exhaust and hurt them. Then they flip them on their backs and eat their quill-less throats and bellies.

According to a recent study in Maine, the state that has the largest fisher population in the eastern United States, adult male fishers have a home range of twelve square miles, while females make do with six, although studies in other states suggest a home range as large as twenty square miles for male fishers. Both sexes establish and defend their territories from others of their sex, but male and female territories overlap in what is called intrasexual territoriality. They live in all forest types although they avoid large openings such as recent clearcuts and farm fields.

Fishers are loners most of their lives, but a female fisher seeks a male in March or April and mates a few days after having her kits. The fertilized egg floats freely in the female's uterus for almost two hundred days before it implants itself in the uterine wall, a process known as delayed implantation. From then on the fetus develops rapidly, and fifty-one weeks after mating the female gives birth to between one and four kits.

The Maine study found that not all female fishers mated or raised kits and that an average of 2.2 kits survived in a litter. Born blind and helpless, they grow slowly, opening their eyes at forty-nine days of age. They are weaned at four months and stay with the female until the fall when they leave to establish their own territories.

Described by one trapper as "a large weasel that looks like a short-legged black fox," the largest males weigh from six to twelve pounds while the females are from four to seven. From their noses to the tips of their long, bushy tails, male fishers measure from thirty-six to forty-eight inches. The smaller females are thirty to thirty-six inches long. They are also darker than the males, sometimes almost coal black. Males are browner with often lighter hairs around their shoulders and faces. Occasionally both sexes have white patches on their necks and throats.

Known colloquially as "black cats" because of their catlike movements, some people even mistake them for black panthers. No one knows why they were named "fishers" because they do not fish for their food. The best guess is that they were originally mistaken for their close relative, the otter, especially since they are also excellent swimmers.

Recently the Pennsylvania Game Commission has released more than one hundred fishers in the northcentral and northeastern part of the state. When I returned home from my walk, I checked the Pennsylvania map to see how far the nearest release site for fishers is from our place. As the crow flies, it is approximately forty miles. Using mostly forested corridors from there to here, it is barely possible that a fisher could end up on our mountain, but it would have had to cross many open valleys and roads including Interstate 80. However, sixteen fishers that were radio-collared dispersed much further than expected, over forty miles in one case. Despite their alleged shyness toward humans, they are also showing up on the few inholdings of private lands in the vast, mostly state-owned forests where they have been released. While getting here may be a problem, we do have ideal fisher habitat and the prey base they need.

I finally concluded that it was barely within the realm of possibility, but that there was not enough evidence to add it to our mammal list for the mountain. Even if it wasn't a fisher, though, it was exciting to know that it could have been. Such a sighting was not even within the realm of possibility before December 1995 when the first Game Commission releases occurred.

JUNE 2. Walking up the Laurel Ridge Trail hill in midmorning, I spotted an animal before it spotted me. I froze in place and used my binoculars to get a close-up look at a gray fox trotting toward me. Finally it stopped and looked intently at me, its ears pricked up. Then it turned aside fearlessly and unhurriedly and walked silently into the woods, as unflappable as all the other gray foxes we have seen here over the years. It was so close that I could see the red on the back of its ears and red on its chest as well as the black stripe on its gray tail streaming out behind it.

I am totally in love with gray foxes, even though rare glimpses are all I ever have of them. Mostly they are crepuscular (active at dusk) and shier than red foxes. They are also handsomer. Their coats are a mixture of red and gray, black and white. The dark, longitudinal stripe along their backs extends as a black mane along the top of their bushy, red and gray tails, hence one of their alternate names, "mane-tailed fox." Other names include "woodfox," "grayback," and "tree fox."

"Tree fox" refers to the unique, tree-climbing ability of the gray fox. It uses the long, sharp, curved claws on its forefeet so that it can grasp and hold onto tree trunks as it shinnies up them, then jumps from branch to branch to escape enemies and forage for food, or settles down to rest. Some even live in hollow trees as high as thirty feet above the ground. Other den sites include hollow logs, rocky outcrops, brush piles, old woodchuck dens, and abandoned outbuildings, all of which must be in densely wooded areas near permanent water.

"Woodfox" aptly describes its habitat preference, deciduous forests such as ours, with rocky terrain and brushy cover. No doubt that is why, when I track them in winter, their tracks go down over the rocky side of Sapsucker Ridge amid a thick cover of mountain laurel and an overstory of mature oaks.

Their food choices vary with the seasons. Primarily meat eaters, they particularly like cottontail rabbits, meadow voles, deer and white-footed mice, shrews, snakes, turtles and their eggs, birds, and insects, especially grasshoppers. In late summer and autumn over a third of their diet consists of vegetable matter such as grasses, apples, wild grapes, acorns, hickory and beechnuts, wild cherries, and corn. They eat more fruits and songbirds than do red foxes because of their tree-climbing ability. They also like deer carrion and often cache food for later consumption.

One year we had a large population of gray foxes. As a result, we saw them more frequently than we ever had before. But first we heard them vocalizing, even in the heat of summer, emitting shrill scream-barks that took us weeks to track down. Such high numbers are a rare occurrence because in addition to death at the hand of humans, they are also killed by great horned owls, red-tailed hawks, domestic dogs, and sometimes coyotes and bobcats. Worst of all, though, are the diseases they are susceptible to—rabies, canine distemper, tularemia, and others, which kill large numbers most years.

Gray foxes mate a little later than red foxes—in late February and early March. Like red foxes, they are monogamous, so not only are the males solicitous toward the females, but they help to care for their offspring. After a gestation period of fifty to sixty days, they produce four to six young in mid-April to early May. The kits are out of the den at four weeks and weaned at eight to twelve weeks. After that, they are ready to accompany their parents on hunting forays. The young disperse by autumn (the record for gray fox travel so far is fifty-one miles from its birthplace) and can reproduce the following February.

The gray fox genus *Urocyon,* meaning "tailed dog," has been here since the Pliocene period (between twelve and two million years ago) and the gray fox itself, *Urocyon cinereoargenteus,* throughout our present Pleistocene period. During the last Ice Age, gray foxes ranged from California to Florida and reached their northernmost limit in Pennsylvania. Remains of gray foxes were common in the excavated pre-Columbian Native American villages in Pennsylvania. Today, sixteen subspecies of gray foxes live from Manitoba and Ontario to northern Venezuela and Colombia. Our subspecies is *U.c. cinereoargenteus,* formerly named *Vulpes Pensylvanicus* (the Pennsylvania fox) because it was discovered in Pennsylvania in 1784, nine years after its initial discovery further south in 1775.

Gray foxes are truly North American mammals, unlike red foxes whom researchers suspect were first brought over by English settlers interested in introducing their tradition of fox hunting with hounds and horses into the New World.

JUNE 3. At 4:40 A.M. one of our trash cans crashed over on the back porch. Grabbing my glasses, I stumbled down in the half-light to find the large black rear end of a bear bent over our washed and crushed tin cans destined for the recycling center. I rushed up to rouse Bruce who, predictably, had slept through the noise directly beneath our bedroom window. He grabbed his camera and groped his way down the stairs. By then the bear had moved forty feet away to our trash burner, but Bruce took a flash photo anyway. Then the bear headed through the grape tangle and along the flat corridor between our yard and the woods. We could hear branches breaking beneath his feet as he moved off. What a way to start the day!

Later, during my walk, I discovered a red-eyed vireo nest hanging from the low branch of a striped maple tree near the Far Field Trail entrance. It contained two porcelain-white, red-eyed vireo eggs, sparsely covered with dark spots, and the aggressively brown-spotted egg of the brown-headed cowbird, notorious for laying its eggs in the nests of others. The red-eyed vireo parent had earlier flushed off the nest as I approached, so I sat down a safe distance from the nest and waited until she returned. She sat on the nest, her head up, the white line above each bright red eye definitive for the red-eyed vireo. The nest, less than four feet from the ground, swayed in the wind like an avian cradle, while the male sang constantly close by. Large striped maple leaves, resembling shiny green umbrellas, sheltered the nest and provided almost perfect camouflage.

Next, while taking a steep side trail bordering our neighbor's property, I found an eastern towhee nest in a blackberry tangle about sixteen inches from the ground. Despite an abundance of towhees on our mountain, this was only the second nest I had ever discovered. It contained two, reddish-purple-splotched, blue eggs and was constructed of oak leaves and grapevines and lined with grass. All the while I examined the nest a towhee called nearby.

Then, coming back through the Far Field thicket, I watched a pair of Kentucky warblers distraction-displaying and calling, but although I searched, I could not find their nest.

I was luckier with a pair of golden-winged warblers. First, they sang lustily. Then they flew closely around me. I walked away for a few minutes, and when I returned, a golden-winged warbler flew up from the ground. Almost immediately I found her nest at the base of a mayapple plant, constructed of dried oak leaves on the outside and lined with grapevines and grasses. The nest contained one brown-headed cowbird egg and one golden-winged warbler egg. The latter was porcelain-white and spotted with orange on its broader end. I must admit that I removed the cowbird egg because although the brown-headed cowbird is a native species, it has been laying its eggs in the nests of birds whose own nestlings are crowded out by the pushier and larger cowbird nestlings. Since cowbirds are overabundant and golden-winged warblers are diminishing, I wanted to give the warblers a chance to raise young without the stress of cowbird foster nestlings.

Finding nests of any kind is not easy. Usually I am lucky to find one nest a week; to find three in one day is as close to a miracle as I can get.

JUNE 4. I headed for the Far Field thicket to check out what I hoped was a red fox den. A couple of hundred feet below the supposed fox den, I found a pile of ruffed grouse feathers that seemed to bear out my suspicions.

Quietly I crept up to the den but instead of foxes, I found a female woodchuck and her youngsters. Because the wind was in my favor and I was half-hidden by sapling leaves, she could not seem to fathom where or what I was. She lived up to her nicknames "whistle pig" and "whistler" as she sat up on her back haunches and emitted a high-pitched whistle, followed by a rapid, nine-syllable, lower trill. Her young immediately went back down into the den.

Despite having seen hundreds of woodchucks over the years, I had never heard this vocalization before. I eased myself from a kneeling to a sitting position and peered through my binoculars at her while she continued her whistling call several dozen times, one every seven seconds. Her head was up and her mouth open so I could see her large incisors. Finally she retreated halfway down her burrow, but she still continued to whistle, a whistle that could be mistaken for the cry of a raptor.

JUNE 5. The last wisps of a heavy June morning fog were evaporating as I started out from the house. Red-winged blackbirds scolded overhead, a male indigo bunting caroled from a tree branch, and a great-crested flycatcher "wheeped" repeatedly.

This was a day I had planned for—totally devoted to wildlife observation—and I saw everything with a heightened sensitivity. I entered the woods, dark and cool, my feet already soaked by the heavy dew. Suddenly I was stopped by the sight of a beautiful insect. Its orange-velvet back, iridescent wings, and fine silver markings were perfect fodder for an artist's brush, but I am no artist. I bent closer to admire its beauty but was repelled by its large, seemingly impersonal, bulbous eyes. Although I could appreciate its beauty aesthetically, I could not empathize with what appeared to be an impersonal insect.

With the wood thrushes empathizing was easy when I discovered two nests woven into mountain laurel shrubs within one hundred feet of each other. At the first nest, the mother sat, alert as usual, her head tilted up in a defiant position. Only at the last moment did she flush, giving me a brief view of three naked, wriggling newborns, incredibly ugly, and one lovely, deep blue, unhatched egg. The newly hatched looked scantily clad with their see-through skins, and I hastily walked away so their mother could return to the nest and brood her helpless young.

The female sat on the edge of the second nest watching both it and me. Only when I reached out as if to touch her did she reluctantly fly to the next bush and wait for me to move on. I looked into the nest and discovered two nestlings sprawled over two more eggs. I left that mother also to her hatching and brooding and continued toward the Far Field, serenaded by two male wood thrushes. Those songsters were probably the new fathers, celebrating the births of their little families, passing out cigars, so to speak.

Eventually, I reached the Far Field—an isolated, overgrown meadow tucked into a deep hollow on the mountaintop. It was flooded with light, but I chose the shady edge of the woods and the furrowed bark of a chestnut oak tree to rest my back against. The branches of the tree reached almost to the ground, a natural camouflage for my still form.

For a while I sat and dozed without moving, letting my consciousness absorb the sounds I heard—American goldfinches burbling overhead, an eastern towhee calling, a train whistling in the distant valley, and, most tantalizing of all, unknown birds singing. Then I was aroused by a rustling beside me. Something was hunting in the leaf mold. I glimpsed a small gray creature as it emerged into the light for a brief second. I waited and watched and every time the wind moved the leaves and changed the pattern of sunlight, I hoped the movement was really the little creature.

The life of a hopeful naturalist is a combination of instant gratification and eternal frustration. Birds sing that I cannot see, flowers bloom that my books don't identify, and incredible unknown insects land on me. I see enough to remain optimistic and hope that I will see more if I am still and patient.

It was a masked shrew! Suddenly it emerged, and its questing nose, its frantic haste, its minute gray body, and long tail made me certain of its identity. It dashed along branches and under leaf mold, its metabolism driving it with nervous speed. Finally it disappeared under the leaf mold, and I doubted that it had even noticed me.

I stood up quietly to stretch. Less than thirty feet away an animal scrambled to its feet and glided silently off through the undergrowth, its large, bushy tail streaming straight out behind it. All the while I had been busily watching the masked shrew on one side of me, a red fox had been lying up on the other side. When had it come? Before me or while I was here? Did it know of my presence? I have read that sometimes foxes like to watch people; they are intrigued by us. Had that been the case or had it been as surprised as I was?

Whatever the case, what I thought was the focus of my hours at the Far Field—the shrew—was a mere sideshow. The red fox had upstaged it. More than any other creature I had seen that day—insect, bird, shrew—I could relate to it. I wondered if it had related in some way, other than fear, to me.

JUNE 6. Nest-watching is one of my major occupations in May and June. Some birds are easier to watch than others, most specifically the cavity nesters such as hairy woodpeckers.

Back in May I had been greeted by loud yells from a female hairy woodpecker as I reached the edge of the Far Field. Apparently I had entered the quarter-acre territory that surrounds the hairy woodpeckers' nest site. All I had to do was find the nest hole.

I had found two other hairy woodpecker nests in as many years, so I knew what to look for. I also tried to hear the nestlings' cries over the cacophony of the female's unremitting alarm calls.

Eventually I located the nest hole forty feet up in the dead branch of a wild black cherry tree. Unlike the nest hole I had discovered in those same woods two years before (also in a black cherry tree branch) this one was easy to see from the ground. Inspired by Margaret Morse Nice's *Watcher at the Nest,* I was determined to learn more about the nest life of hairy woodpeckers, so I settled down against a comfortable tree trunk a safe (for the birds) forty feet away and trained my binoculars on the nest hole.

For the next nine mornings, I spent a couple of hours each day watching the nest. I compared what I saw with what I had seen at other nests and with what other woodpecker observers had recorded. I knew from my reading that, once again, I had discovered a nest in the second half of its twenty-eight-to-thirty-day nestling phase.

Hairy woodpeckers—who mate for life—begin courting in midwinter, calling and drumming within their six-to-eight-acre, year-round range. They drum on resonant trees known as "signal posts." Each bird has two to four separate posts, and both males and females use drumming to assert their presence on their territory and to bring back their mates; they lead separate lives in fall and early winter.

Once pair bonds are reestablished, there is a lull until nest excavation begins in mid-April. Then the male does most of the nest-building; his bill is 10 percent longer than the female's and better equipped for digging into the wood. Copulation takes place during nest building and egg laying and is always initiated by the female.

After four to six white eggs are laid on a soft bed of wood chips at the bottom of the ten- to fifteen-inch-deep nest cavity, the parents share incubation duties. They alternate frequently during the daytime, but the male incubates throughout the night while the female retires to a nearby roost hole.

Throughout the eleven- to twelve-day incubation period, the woodpeckers are silent. From my observations, at least, they remain quiet until the second half of the nestling phase. That is when they switch from entering the nest hole while feeding the nestlings to feeding from the outside. At sixteen days of age, the nestlings can climb up to the nest entrance; the parents land on the branch and poke their bills crammed full of insects into the chirping youngsters' wide-open bills.

Chirp they do—incessantly, unendingly, piercingly—leading me straight to their nest hole. In addition to the loud protest cries of their parents, which usually lasted ten minutes or more whenever I entered their territory, the parents always announced their impending arrival at the nest hole with far-off calls. These calls induced their nestlings to chirp even louder. Not only did the parents—particularly the female—keep up their alarm calls every day I watched, but occasionally they would land on nearby trees and drum, protesting my presence with what researcher Lawrence Kilham in his book *Woodpeckers of Eastern North America* calls "demonstrative drumming."

Often the female was torn between food gathering and protesting, but as the days passed, the length of her protests diminished from ten minutes to two. That occurred at the same time that both parents stepped up their feedings to every five minutes, five days before the young fledged.

Six days previously, I had finally seen a nestling at the nest hole. It jabbed at the female as she landed on the branch, and she reared back her head before flying off.

Four days later one nestling stuck its head completely out of the hole each time it was fed. Yesterday it sat silently looking out of the hole in between feedings.

Today I arrived at 9 A.M. A nestling was halfway out of the hole, calling the adult woodpecker's "peek-peek" and trilling instead of making the usual chirping noises. In and out its head popped like a jack-in-the-box. It was still a fuzzy juvenile with a grayish-white throat and chest, but it had white and black on its head.

Nearly an hour after I arrived, a parent flew in, remained near the tree a minute or two without feeding the youngster, and then flew off. Another hour passed and no parent appeared, even though the nestling protested and called most of the time.

Kilham says that hairies have two methods of enticing young from the nest. One is to hold food just out of their reach, forcing them to lean out a little too far, and the other is to starve them, making them so hungry that they tumble out. This nestling seemed to be getting the starvation treatment.

I waited more than two hours and finally had to leave. Once again I'd missed the fledging. But because hairy woodpeckers are abundant, year-round residents here, I know I will have many more opportunities to add to my store of hairy woodpecker nest observations in the years to come.

JUNE 7. Another cavity nester I've been watching is the white-breasted nuthatch. Not much is known about the nest life of white-breasted nuthatches because they usually nest in high tree cavities. So I was thrilled early this spring not only to find a white-breasted nuthatch nest but to have the opportunity to observe it.

Early on the morning of April 20 I sat in the woods absorbing the sounds and sights of awakening spring. Suddenly I noticed a white-breasted nuthatch gathering shredded bark from a red maple tree. Then it flew three feet to a small dead tree with the top broken but still attached and disappeared on the far side of the broken top. The tree was about twenty feet from the edge of First Field, so I walked into the field behind the tree and spotted a rotted knothole in it, a favorite nesting site for nuthatches. The nest hole was six and a quarter inches wide, ten feet from the ground, and faced north.

The next day I watched a nuthatch sweeping its bill back and forth on the bark near the nest hole, a sure sign that I had located a nuthatch nest. Bill-sweeping is performed by both parents several days in a row, for ten minutes, usually before and after periods of nest-building. Later, during incubation and nestling periods, bill-sweeping occurs in late afternoon.

Sometimes the birds have crushed insects in their bills when they bill-sweep and, scientists believe, they are using the chemical defense secretions emitted by the insects to discourage squirrels from entering the nest. Researcher Lawrence Kilham discovered that a pair of nuthatches in his aviary used blister beetles, which exude an oily blistering fluid, to sweep their nest site.

Other researchers report that nuthatches often use smelly materials in their nests as well. One observer reported finding the lining of a nest made up almost exclusively of nicotine-laden filters from cigarette butts. Other times the birds stuff bits of fur in bark crevices surrounding the nest hole.

Knowing that the female lays an average of eight eggs and that the incubation period is about fourteen days, I waited until May 28 to begin watching the nest hole. At 7:00 P.M. I settled down about twenty feet from the nest tree. Both parents silently came and went, feeding the nestlings, a refreshing contrast to the noisy hairy woodpeckers. They always landed up or down the limb from the nest hole and then scuttled along the limb and into the hole.

When a parent entered the nest the young called quietly. Then the parent would emerge with a fecal sac in its bill and fly off. White-breasted nuthatches are scrupulously clean, keeping not only their nests free of fecal matter but their own roost holes, which they occupy throughout the year.

Each day since then I have spent quiet time watching the comings and goings of the parents. Once, when I moved closer to the nest tree, a parent froze in place, upside down, outside the nest hole, and did not move until I returned to my usual watching post.

On June 1, between 7:24 and 7:29 P.M., the parents fed the nestlings five times. Caterpillars were favorite food items and they looked like they were tent caterpillars. Moths were another frequently fed item.

To sit, day after day, watching a nuthatch nest has its special privileges. One evening I was serenaded by a scarlet tanager, black-billed cuckoo, indigo bunting, and rose-breasted grosbeak. I also listened to the syncopated bass drumming of a pileated woodpecker. Late on another morning I enjoyed a day of light and shadow as clouds raced across the blue sky and the wind rippled the field grasses. A pair of turkey vultures soared overhead and eastern bluebirds and northern cardinals sang.

Probably the best day was June 4 when, as I walked across First Field headed for the nest, I spotted the perked-up ears and alert face of a doe looking at me intently from her bed in the grasses. I started toward her and she leaped reluctantly away, a signal to me that a fawn was nearby. And so it was, nestled in the grasses, its nose wet and questing, its legs bent back under it. No more than a day old, it trembled when I bent down to speak to it. Not wishing to prolong its fright, I moved quickly away. At the nest site itself, Baltimore orioles, Acadian flycatchers, and great-crested flycatchers sang. Chipmunks scampered in the dry leaves and gray squirrels foraged in the leaf duff.

Sometimes when I arrived at the nest site, the parents would utter a few, faint "yank-yanks," but usually they were quiet. Occasionally a parent would land near the hole and look about for a minute or so before going into the nest to feed. Once a parent bird sat peering out of the entrance for several seconds before emerging onto the limb, walking slowly up it, looking carefully around, and then flying off. Clearly they were on the lookout for predators.

On June 5 the young were piping softly not only when a parent flew in with food but long after the parent left the nest. By then the adults were taking only about a minute to adjust to my arrival.

Ominously today, though, they have changed their behavior. At first one parent looked as if it was ready to feed but was scared off by my arrival. The other one "yank-yanked" a couple of times before it also flew away. At 10:14 a parent with a caterpillar in its beak paraded up and down the upper side of the nest hole limb but would not go into the nest. The other parent perched in a nearby tree.

Then the parent with the caterpillar also flew to a nearby tree, called softly, and flew back to the nest hole limb while the other adult remained on a nearby tree. Both hesitated, protested softly, and flew off. At 10:26 they still refused to enter the nest hole, and I heard no sound from the nestlings. Once I watched a parent fly directly at a gray squirrel climbing a tree near the nest tree. Had it killed the nestlings?

Something obviously had. I mourned the loss of the little family. "Nature's way," my rational mind said. "But why that particular little family?" my heart protested.

As solace for that loss, I sat up in the woods nearby and had a close-up view of courting and mating gray squirrels. A dozen or more in three different groups chased and grunted. Several females were in heat at the same time, so as each appeared, she was chased by a varying number of males.

Then, as many as five males at a time chased a smaller female to within eight feet of me. She let only one of them close enough to sniff her rear end. After that he followed her as if enslaved, his nose close to her behind. Apparently this privilege was a signal to the rest of the males that she had made her choice, because they sat or lay out flat on the ground and waited, but they continued their grunting noises. Finally the pair mated on the ground in front of me. Although all the squirrels clearly saw me sitting there, they were too busy courting and mating to care.

Later, at 12:55 P.M., as I was preparing lunch, Mark looked out our bow window and called to his wife Luz and me, "Oso!" Even I knew what that word meant in Spanish. We rushed to the window and watched as a large black bear walked beneath the first apple tree in the flat area below the house and looked up at it as if in search of apples.

Luz was tremendously excited. Having lived in Honduras most of her life, she had never seen a bear and had listened skeptically to our bear stories. She ran outside to stand on our back porch and get an even closer view, talking volubly in Spanish, while Mark whistled at the bear. It showed no sign that it heard or saw us but ambled on to the next small apple tree, where it paused for a few seconds. Then it moved to the last apple tree and reached up into its branches as if marking it. Finally the bear walked up into the woods of Laurel Ridge and disappeared from our view.

Luz was still marveling over her sighting several hours later and eagerly told her story to Bruce and David in halting English. "Bear" was one of her first spoken English words.

JUNE 8. There is a place on our mountain where I almost always see wildlife no matter what the time or season. I call it "the magic place." Along with having all the elements wildlife needs to survive—food, water, and shelter—it is also serenely beautiful.

Growing on this two-acre plot are nineteen tree species of various sizes and ages. Counting the rings on some stumps, I found trees that dated back to 1815. The few huge red oaks and white oaks still standing probably started growing about the same time.

The oaks are found among the smaller mockernut and pignut hickories, numerous white ashes, a solitary white pine, one of only two butternuts on our property, venerable black gums, and red and sugar maples. The understory is made up of witch hazel, striped maple, and spicebush.

This is edge habitat at its best. Bounded by the overgrown First Field on the northwest and a small power line right-of-way on the northeast, the half-mile strip of woods extends southeastward over the crest of Laurel Ridge and down to the fields of Sinking Valley. Looking southwest, the first road break occurs after nearly four miles of mostly unbroken forest, providing refuge for a diverse number of birds and mammals.

Some wild creatures live in the magic place year-round; many more use the area for food and water only, judging by the network of tracks leading in and out during the winter. They funnel across First Field from Sapsucker Ridge and down from the drier heights of Laurel Ridge. Still others use it as a quick stopover during migration.

Today strange owl-like cries emanated from the magic place and drew me to sit quietly beneath a tree to listen. Through the thick leaf canopy I glimpsed what I thought was a fluffy, brownish-beige bird fly into the top of a nearby large oak tree, but after a long wait, I neither saw nor heard anything more.

Finally I wandered a few hundred feet away and nearly stepped on a young, gray phase, eastern screech owl sitting on the ground. It swiveled its head around as I moved and talked quietly to it. Then I sat down ten feet away at the base of a tree and watched to see if a parent would come in. Surely the "wooing" cries I had heard earlier had been from this little one.

The juvenile owl remained alert, looking small and brave and utterly self-possessed, as owls always do. After a short spell of bravado, it seemed to accept my presence and kept blinking hard in an effort to stay awake. Several times it puffed itself into a fluffy ball and closed its eyes for a few seconds.

According to the *Atlas of Breeding Birds of Pennsylvania,* eastern screech owls are found in all areas of the commonwealth, and 75 percent of them are gray colored. The other 25 percent are a bright red-brown. They are cavity nesters who prefer to refurbish the old nest cavities of northern flickers or pileated woodpeckers, instead of building new nests, with meager bits of wood chips, dead leaves, and fur and feathers from their prey.

Nests have been found from five up to eighty feet above the ground. In them the owls lay their two to seven glossy white eggs in late winter or early spring. In this case, I estimated that the female had started laying eggs in late March since incubation is thirty days and the nestling phase another four weeks.

Apparently fledglings cannot fly well when they leave the nest, but they can climb by using their bills, talons, and wings. At this period, the female is said to be protective and to swoop down on intruders such as me. Yet although I sat there for nearly an hour, no parent appeared.

Finally, I slipped off to bring back my family for a look. When we returned to the magic place, the little owl was gone.

JUNE 9. As I set out on my walk this morning, three gray catbirds tried to out-sing each other in the lilac bush as they competed for territory. A female eastern bluebird gathered huge beaksful of cut grass for her new nest in the box nailed to a power pole at the edge of First Field.

Along Laurel Ridge Trail I pursued an unknown bird call. It sounded like a bird of prey and led me on a merry chase for a quarter-mile. No matter how I tried I could not see it.

Finally it called again off in the underbrush. I walked ten feet into the woods and sat there, my back against a small tree, determined to wait out the hidden bird. Having recently reread W. H. Hudson's *Green Mansions,* I felt a little like the narrator of the book, Abel, who was led deeper and deeper into the forest by the warbling calls of what he thought was some exotic bird but turned out to be the mysterious heroine, Rima.

The bird that had tantalized me neither called again nor appeared. Instead I heard a rustle over my right shoulder and, by turning slowly, did not startle the doe eating on the other side of a laurel bush about six feet from where I sat. Reluctant to break the spell, I remained still.

Gradually I became aware of another kind of noise, that of an animal moving through the underbrush off to my left. It sounded like none of the creatures' movements I can usually identify—turkey, squirrel, deer—so I stayed still, my hopes rising with every heavy footfall.

Sure enough, a black bear emerged from a tangle of laurel bushes thirty-five feet in front of my tree and paused to sniff the air several times. The doe, who had continued grazing on the other side of the laurel bush, snorted once and bolted.

The bear lowered its head between two chestnut oak trees and raised it again with what looked like slobber dripping from its mouth. Then it reared up on its hind legs and peered nearsightedly in my direction. Except for a touch of cinnamon on its face, the bear was shiny black and looked as if it weighed a few hundred pounds, not the biggest black bear I had ever seen but certainly the closest.

Even though I was sitting on Laurel Ridge, named for the mountain laurel that blankets the area, no laurel or underbrush of any kind grew between the bear and me. So when it started ambling directly toward me, my mind did a quick calculation. Intellectually I reasoned that black bears are harmless and run when they see humans. On the other hand, by my figuring, that bear had a good chance of stepping on me. Even a peaceful bear, when startled, might swat first.

So, with the bear a mere twenty-five feet away, I reluctantly abandoned my watching and slowly stood up. The bear halted, then spun around and dashed off. Except for an elevated heartbeat and slightly wobbly legs, my chief feeling was one of elation that I had had such an intimate glimpse of a black bear.

Curious about what had attracted the bear to the two chestnut oaks, I walked over and discovered that they were joined at the base and had a pool of water in the hollow between them. The bear had been drinking, not slobbering.

Exhilarated by my close encounter, I continued my walk down Laurel Ridge Trail. Close to the intersection of Laurel Ridge and First Field trails, that same bear jumped up from where it had been resting, off the right side of the trail under a laurel bush twenty feet away, and ran across First Field. This time it had seen me before I saw it—tit for tat.

Then, next to the Far Field Road, a fawn leaped up from where it had been watching me and dashed up the slope. A few seconds later, another took off three feet from me. Those fawns reacted like I had with the bear, only they had waited until I was even closer than the bear had been to me before their nerve broke.

JUNE 10. Once again I walked to the magic place and was not disappointed. An eastern chipmunk emerged from her burrow and gathered dead leaves only five feet from where I was situated. She pushed leaves into her cheek pouches while sitting up on her haunches.

Then she zipped back into her burrow. In a couple of minutes she was out again. This time she paused to watch me intently for several minutes and then stretched her body as far as she could to gather more dead leaves in her cheek pouches before diving back into her burrow.

I suspected she was building a nest for her young, but according to Joseph Merritt's *Guide to the Mammals of Pennsylvania,* her timing was way out of sync. Summer litters, which occur after a thirty-one-day gestation period, usually are born in mid-to-late August.

A chipmunk nest, however, is constructed of chewed or crushed leaves, and as she made trip after collecting trip, I had no doubt that she was building a nest. She probably had lost her first litter and was trying for a second one ahead of most chipmunk females, who would normally still have their first family under their care.

The longer I sat there, the more she went in and out of her burrow and traveled farther to gather leaves, as if she was finally trusting me. The fifth time she emerged, she scolded a couple of notes before sitting and watching me, perfectly still and camouflaged, for many minutes. Then she resumed tearing at big leaves—chewing them into pieces, pulling, yanking, and stretching high on her haunches, gathering still more material.

All the while the breeze blew, and light and shadow played over the forest floor. Scarlet tanagers, eastern wood pewees, eastern towhees, a blue-gray gnatcatcher, red-eyed vireo, indigo bunting, American redstart, and black-billed cuckoo sang, sometimes in turn, sometimes two or three at the same time.

On her sixth trip, the chipmunk immediately started to gather leaves and even turned her back to me. Then she was in and out rapidly, gathering leaves with nervous haste, her mouth stretched in a wide grimace by the bulky material. It was amazing how much she could stuff into her pouches. The next time she also took a small twig.

On her eighth emergence, she was put briefly on alert by distant "chips" from another chipmunk and stopped to listen. Perceiving no threat to herself, she continued her gathering and popped back down her burrow.

Reluctant to betray her growing trust in me, I waited until she went down into her burrow with still another load before rising, stretching my stiff body, and continuing on my way.

As I walked along the Short Circuit Trail, I heard what sounded like desperate calls from downy woodpeckers. I tracked the noisemakers down and found a pair flying in agitation around a tall dead tree. A black snake had its head in the woodpecker nesting hole and was eating the young woodpeckers. I could see the bulges they made in the snake's sleek body.

The parents flew in repeatedly, diving close but never touching the snake. A male scarlet tanager landed on the same bare tree branch where the parents displayed, as if lending them moral support in their uneven match with the bird-eating snake.

When the snake pulled its head out of the hole and looked around for a few minutes, the parents slackened the intensity and volume of their calls, but they still persisted as they swooped above and to the side of the snake. All the while the snake seemed impervious to their protests and, after a few minutes, put its head back into the hole. Again the parents called louder and flew closer.

Gradually their protests diminished. Finally the female flew off, leaving the male to call halfheartedly as the snake finished its meal.

From the imminent birth of chipmunks to the quick death of downy woodpecker nestlings in the space of a few hundred feet, the magic place had once again provided me with glimpses of the usually secretive lives of wild animals.

JUNE 11. This morning I sat, my back against a large black cherry tree at the edge of the Far Field, peering out from the greenish light of the forest at the sun-flooded tableau of the field. A breeze carried all the evocative, warm odors of summer—essence of rose and humus and green grass. Patches of light shone greenly down through the tropical-forest-like canopy. I am wedded to the green hills of Pennsylvania, to filtered light and bright fields dancing with butterflies, a benign setting where there is little fear of serpents or thirst or blinding heat and few threats from insects or larger wild animals.

Then I heard the maniacal cry of a pileated woodpecker. He swooped in low like a dive bomber, skillfully zooming around trees despite his crow size, and finally landed about thirty feet behind me to work on a fallen tree trunk. Slowly I pivoted myself around to watch as he flung large pieces of bark several feet in the air in search of carpenter ants, the piece de resistance for pileated woodpeckers. For half an hour he moved about and around the dead log, hopping awkwardly on the forest floor. His red mustache on his black and white face and red forehead beneath his magnificent red crest identified him as a male pileated. Never had I watched the usually wary pileated woodpecker undetected and at such close range.

Then, to cap off the experience, a gray squirrel hopped up to the pileated and chased him to a nearby tree branch about a foot from the ground. The woodpecker spread his flashing black and white wings in protest but, undeterred, the squirrel rushed at him, forcing the pileated to fly to another low tree branch. I expected further aggression from the squirrel, but instead it hopped off with what seemed an insouciant air, content to have rattled the woodpecker by displaying its dominance over the imposing bird.

Later, as I sat in the kitchen eating my lunch, I heard continual scolding from birds but could not see any threat to them. Then I heard a pileated woodpecker calling on and on at the edge of the woods, so I went outside to investigate. A red-tailed hawk took off low to the ground heading straight down the hollow and instantly the pileated quieted. I could not see if the hawk had anything in its talons. So much is hidden now, at this time of year, both predator and prey, and it is difficult to interpret what I hear.

At 2:25 P.M., I glanced out the upstairs hall window and watched one woodchuck chase another up the driveway, grab it briefly, and try to tussle while the victim broke away and tore across the lawn toward the grape tangle. The aggressor, a darker, somewhat larger woodchuck than usual, ran halfway across the lawn in pursuit, then reared up on its haunches to look around before lowering itself and trotting back to the driveway and up beyond the garage. I presumed this was some kind of territorial dispute or perhaps it was a mother chasing off her young since, by now, those born in early April would be on their own.

JUNE 12. I was outside early, sitting on the veranda, watching and listening to frenzied birds singing, chasing, calling, and scolding, as if the humidity had lubricated their voice boxes. A gray catbird sang his nonstop improvisations in the forsythia bushes; a pair of great-crested flycatchers rose together in the sky, chasing and then clashing briefly, beak to beak. Barn swallows dipped and swayed over the billowing grasses of First Field.

A female ruby-throated hummingbird buzzed on to the veranda, examined the windows and shutters, and flew close to where I sat on the rocker. Finally she hesitated on swirling wings near my crossed feet and I had a superb view of her iridescent green back. Since my moccasins and socks were dark brown and my pants green, I could only imagine that she was paying a neighborly visit instead of buzzing me as hummingbirds sometimes do when I wear red.

During my morning walk, the woods dripped with water from past storms, fog, and heavy dew, our own seasonal rain forest. Both Eva and Luz thrive in this tropical weather. Although the birds are already fledging, Eva is still mostly eating and sleeping, requiring total care—yet she tries to talk, she smiles, and when she is fussy, a walk outside in someone's arms calms her down.

Later I hitched a ride to the bottom of the mountain with Bruce and walked up the hollow road. An Acadian flycatcher began scolding, so I followed her with my binoculars until she gave away her nest site at the end of an American beech tree branch overhanging the road about ten feet from the ground. Her nest habitat exactly suits the description in the *Atlas of Breeding Birds in Pennsylvania,* which says the Acadian flycatcher "inhabits woodlands near streams, where it frequently builds in the pendant branches of a beech" (200). I was absolutely elated to have found a nest after hearing the bird singing in the hollow for three summers. Best of all, it was not only a new breeding bird for the mountain but for the county as well.

JUNE 13. Birds were everywhere during my morning walk. An ovenbird performed its distraction display along the Guesthouse Trail. A female yellow-breasted chat sounded an alarm when I crossed the power line right-of-way. The woods along the Far Field Road were filled with common grackles. Yellow-billed cuckoos called loudly. The red-eyed vireo nest contained one hatched young and two unhatched eggs, including the brown-headed cowbird's. Among the bird singers and callers in and around the Far Field environs were a wood thrush, indigo bunting, scarlet tanager, great-crested flycatcher, ovenbird, worm-eating warbler, American robin, and field sparrow.

This morning the woods beside the Far Field also rustled with squirrels and chipmunks. First a gray squirrel scampered past, then a chipmunk, and finally a fox squirrel. The latter stopped and sniffed in the leaf duff as if searching for buried nuts. If it saw me sitting ten feet from where it was foraging, it did not act alarmed but continued on its slow, methodical way. A doe, whom I approached from the rear, nursed twins on the Sapsucker Ridge Trail sixty-five feet away and directly in front of me. At first only one fawn nursed. It stood beneath her and faced her tail. The other fawn foraged on the trail ahead. Then it too scampered back and nursed, facing in the same direction. There seemed to be no competition or shoving between the two. When I tried to ease myself down to the ground to watch, the fawns spotted me. They ran ahead, looking back, which made the doe glance around, take a couple of steps forward, stamp, and then run in the direction her fawns had. I was impressed with the fawns' alertness at such an early age.

There is an unusually high population of froghoppers on the weeds and grasses this year, so walking across the top of First Field quickly soaked my pants as I waded through hundreds of "houses of bubbles" as Edwin Way Teale calls them in his book *Near Horizons.* Each bubble consists of plant tissues' sap that the froghopper sucks up with its pointed beak as food. The excess liquid, mixed with chemicals from tiny glands in the insect and whipped by its tail as it emerges out of the end of its abdomen, flows downward over its body and covers it in foam. Because of its chemical makeup—a waxy enzyme and an alkali—it is like a natural soap, which increases both the viscosity of the liquid and the endurance of the bubbles. Those bubbles can last as long as a week without hardening or evaporating.

As I walked down First Field Trail, my ears were filled with the singing of rose-breasted grosbeaks, both from within those woods and across on Sapsucker Ridge. Amazing how I can walk in and out of zones of birdsong, sometimes of only one or two species, other times of six species or more, interspersed with pockets that seem to be birdless.

A gray fox crossed the trail where it meets the Short Circuit Trail, sniffed a fallen log, and then trotted back across the trail and into First Field, turning once in my direction so that I had a good look at it, but it did not see me.

JUNE 14. I walked down the road this morning and aroused the first distraction display of the year by a Louisiana waterthrush along the road bank, although I could not find the nest.

Down near the bottom of the road, a fledgling fluttered up from the side and then barely flew far enough to make it down the hill a few feet from where I stood. At first I thought it was a young rose-breasted grosbeak. As it sat on the ground, fluffed up and peeping loudly, a female scarlet tanager flew in and fed it barely ten feet from me. That mottled brown fledgling, blending in with the woods' floor, bore no resemblance to its flamboyant male parent, nor did it look like the yellow-breasted, green-backed female.

The fledgling fluttered up to a branch barely a foot above the ground and continued peeping while the female came in to feed it two more times before she spotted me watching. She flew to a nearby rhododendron bush and scolded and then on to a nearby tree before flying off. Her scolding was enough to quiet the fledgling. After a couple of minutes, the adult returned to scold and watched me again from a low hemlock snag. Her continual calling brought in the male to scold, along with a worm-eating warbler. The female flew within a few feet of me, the male hung back farther, and the worm-eating warbler stayed on the periphery. More and more birds gathered. The fledgling remained frozen and quiet on the branch while pandemonium erupted around it. Even an eastern wood pewee called several times as if in sympathy. Not wishing to draw a real predator to the scene, I quickly moved on up the hollow, accompanied by a steady parade of red-spotted purple butterflies pumping their wings in the sunlit patches of the road, as many as half a dozen in only a few yards.

Near 6:00 P.M. I looked out the kitchen door and saw our resident bear heading toward the driveway from the flat area. It paused to eat near the first apple tree. Mark, Luz, and Eva stood on the guest house front porch watching as it walked down the driveway and out of sight. So close had they been to it that they could see a white mark on its chest—just like one of the bears who had invaded our back porch last autumn.

JUNE 15. As usual, a house finch family occupied one nest in a recess on top of a veranda column and an eastern phoebe another. Yesterday two of the four house finch nestlings fledged. Today I watched a third one leave as I sat at the hall window. The father was not feeding them but instead was flying to a nearby column capitol with food in his beak. This so excited one fledgling that it flew over to the column, but the parent left without feeding it. Back the nestling flew to the nest. Both nestlings then kept up an insistent hollering.

Again the male flew in with something in his beak, then left the nest still carrying the "bait," followed by the third nestling. The fourth continued hollering, so one of the phoebe parents sitting on their nest flew over and fed the house finch nestling. After more hollering, the house finch nestling was silent for a while and seemed to be dozing. Then it resumed a quieter complaining but no parent appeared. Near dusk the nest was finally empty.

JUNE 16. I sat on the veranda before seven this morning. Suddenly I heard a strange "scritching" noise coming, I thought, from the old garden area. Still in bathrobe and slippers, I wandered through the upper yard and saw nothing. The strange noise persisted so I walked up the driveway. As I started past the old garden site, I spotted a large, male black bear shredding the wood of the power pole on the right-of-way, pulling off long splinters, his back toward me. Next he turned around and rubbed his back sensuously over the pole, his head lolling back, the bottoms of his paws visible. Circling around behind the pole, he "scritched" some more. Then he broke down and mouthed a sapling beside the pole. Finally, he lumbered across to the small patch of woods beside the old garden. I watched as he made his slow way on a diagonal, stopping occasionally to look at something briefly, then moving on. He never saw my still figure standing there and watching him.

As he moved down the slope and briefly out of sight, I walked down the driveway and through the backyard where I could look down at the flat area below. I was just in time to see him break off and mouth an apple tree branch from the old tree there. Then he stood up on his hind legs, facing me, and I noticed he had that same large, white, somewhat heart-shaped mark on his chest. Finally he ambled the length of the level area to the driveway, across the road grate, and out of sight down the hollow road. All the while I had stood in plain view, holding my coffee mug, and watched his progress, but he never once looked up toward the house. Several birds in the grape tangle scolded as he plodded past in his flat-footed way. I stood, jubilant, excited, and thankful that I had been able to watch him unobserved from beginning to end, a wild black bear going about his business as usual.

Later, I inspected the power pole and discovered that the bear could reach several inches higher than I could—a little over six feet. The area around the pole was trampled down and there was a pile of shredded pole splinters on the ground, one of which was a foot and a half long. Once again he had been marking his territory during mating season.

The rest of my day was anticlimactic as I sat in the magic place and was serenaded by a wood thrush who flew in closer than usual and allowed himself to be seen. On the Dump Trail I found a yellow-and-brown-shelled eastern box turtle at the junction with the Short Circuit Trail. It sat, its head out of its shell, watching me carefully while I watched it for a while.

Unlike black bears, box turtles see very well and I have yet to surprise one.

JUNE 17. Most of the birds' nests I have been observing have successfully fledged. I watched the three American robins leave their mud-lined nest in the lilac bush. Then I saw the six guest house portico eastern phoebes sail out from the ledge in all directions. The following day the five garage phoebes took off.

This morning, as I ate breakfast, I watched a parent common crow foraging on our lawn accompanied by two fledglings as large as their parent. They fluttered their wings and cried "waa-waa" like babies as they begged for food. For the most part the parent ignored them even when chased by the young.

The chipping sparrows have also had a mostly successful season so far. The four corn crib chipping sparrows had fledged before 7:30 A.M. yesterday, but today I caught the last act of the herb garden chipping sparrow fledging. I heard the mother chipping and went out to find the most timid nestling clinging determinedly to a branch of the juniper bush while its mother called from the grape tangle.

My appearance tipped the balance and the nestling quickly changed into a fledgling by flying into the side of the house, picking itself up off the ground, and then sailing precariously down into the grape tangle.

Another successful fledging I attended was that of the four gray catbirds in the barberry hedge. While the parents scolded, I watched the young step from their nest and plunge out into the world. The second catbird nest I discovered was in the lilac bush, and as I tried to peer into it, a nestling hopped out just as both parents flew in close, screaming their rage at me, so I left them in peace.

Halfway up the Guesthouse Trail a worm-eating warbler began to scold me and, following its cue, I turned into the woods. The farther in I went, searching for a nest that was supposed to be on the ground, the more distressed the worm-eating warbler became.

Finally it threw itself on the ground, stomach down, and flipped its tail from side to side, all the while making distress noises in its distraction display. I never did find the nest, but later I learned that I had been watching the display of a female worm-eating warbler whose nestlings are close to fledging.

It continued to be a morning for excitable parents: when I reached the power line right-of-way, a male golden-winged warbler gave his distraction display. Then a black-and-white warbler flew down into a bush with a worm and reappeared without it. Along the Laurel Ridge Trail a female hooded warbler scolded while the male grasped a fat caterpillar in his beak and flew off.

JUNE 18. I walked to the Far Field thicket and quietly approached from the rear a red fox den I had recently discovered. I had little hope of seeing anything, but as I moved to within fifteen feet of the entrance, a fox pup emerged and looked straight at me. I knew it had seen me so I talked quietly to it for five minutes as it continued watching, sniffing, and easing slowly out from the hole to stand on all four of its black legs and look at me. What an exquisite creature! How rewarded I felt, being the closest I have ever been to a pup.

Over the years, when I have unexpectedly encountered a wild creature, I have always spoken to it, a practice, I recently learned, that naturalist and writer Bernd Heinrich also engages in. We have both discovered that we can, for a short time, charm such creatures with our voices. So it was today. Over and over I told the pup how beautiful it was, asked it where its siblings were, promised that I wouldn't hurt it, and made other similar nonthreatening remarks. All the while it watched me with what seemed like curiosity, not fear. Probably it was too young to have learned a fear of humans.

When at last it retreated back into its den, I continued on my way to sit at the base of my favorite black cherry tree in the Far Field woods. More and more chipmunks congregated nearby, unusual behavior for this normally solitary creature. Then, off to one side, a pair mated. During the several minutes they remained paired, he on top of her and actively thrusting while she was still, he nibbled around her ears. Then a third chipmunk rushed up, all three tumbled in a brief skirmish, and finally they rushed off in opposite directions.

In the evening Bruce and I waited until 9:30 to walk down the hollow road in the dark and look at the foxfire David recently discovered. We found the roots of an overturned tree trunk glowing with what seemed like an inner light. On the ground were more pieces of foxfire. Bruce broke off several and I carried them up in my hands, put them in a dish, and let them glow in our bedroom all night. In ordinary light all that is visible is the white, rotting inner bark of a tree, but in the dark the mycelium of *Armillaria mellea,* the honey mushroom, glows. Had we continued to pull the bark apart we would have found more foxfire. Bioluminescence, or emission of light from living organisms, is the result of internal oxidative changes. Its eerie but beautiful light deserves to be classified with stories of elves abroad on dark nights.

Mycelium are the tangle of threads or spawn of the mushroom spores cast off by the fruiting bodies and used to produce more mushrooms. Because they are microscopic we could not actually see them with the naked eye when we looked at the bark. It is not the root system of a mushroom but the plant itself that has been developed to produce and scatter more spores. When conditions of moisture and heat are right, it grows and feeds on whatever substances it happens to be invading and later forms a mushroom. The honey mushroom or oak fungus is considered edible but it is nicknamed the "white plague of trees" because it causes oak root rot by working on the roots and sapwood under the bark and

killing the tree. After removing the bark of a tree afflicted
with the *Armillaria* disease, one can pull loose long, black
cords of compacted mycelium by means of which the trouble
is carried into further feeding grounds, according to Louis C.
C. Krieger in *The Mushroom Handbook*. He calls it the shoe-
string disease. I wonder if, by removing the bark and bringing it home, we have spread the disease? On the other hand,
Orson K. Miller Jr. in his *Mushrooms of North America* claims
that only "under certain, as yet unknown, conditions, [is] this
fungus capable of becoming a virulent parasite." He also calls
it a choice mushroom, "one of the best edibles" (107). What a
world of complexity there is in a single mushroom species.
No wonder scientists fret about the rapidly accelerating loss
of biodiversity. So much knowledge about the natural world
is being heedlessly lost, never to be recovered.

JUNE 19. A flaming sun rose at six in the morning, a
warning of the heat to come, so I was out walking by seven.
By then it was already oppressively hot even though I wore
only shorts and a tank top. Because of the singing gnats, I
walked rapidly down the road to the bridge. The black gum
tree along the edge of the woods, displaying shining, elliptic
leaves with drip tips, looked as tropical as the weather felt.
Despite the heat, gray squirrels energetically chased each other. Two deer bounded off. Chipmunks foraged in the leaf
duff. The bird chorus of early dawn was already fading except
for wood thrushes, Acadian flycatchers, black-and-white and
worm-eating warblers, ovenbirds, and eastern towhees.

I was home in an hour, my glasses steaming as I tried to
drink the last of my coffee for the day and eat Bruce's whole
wheat/buckwheat blueberry pancakes with maple syrup.
David returned from a walk over to Margaret's old yard to say
how beautiful it looked with the catalpa trees blooming and a
rainbow splash of sweet Williams blanketing the earth beneath. Even as the old house decays and molders, its front

door gaping open, its porch roof collapsing, the yard grows more wild and beautiful.

Never have the wood thrushes been so tuneful. From dawn until dusk, even during the heat of midday, they sing on and on. I can hear them inside with the fan on at noon at ninety degrees. I have always thought of them as dawn and dusk singers, only singing all day when it is wet and dark, but they, like all the birds in this weather, seem hyped up rather than stunned, as we are, by the unrelenting, pressing heat.

JUNE 20. On May 19, 1990, I made a momentous discovery in a grove of red maple trees at the edge of the Far Field—a new orchid species for the mountain. For nearly twenty years, the only orchid species we had was the pink lady's slipper. Then, a pair of large, round, shiny green leaves appeared, only one plant, I discovered, as I carefully searched the area. Until it actually blossomed, in late June, I was not certain of its species, but once the flower stalk bloomed with greenish-white blossoms, I was. We were the proud owners of one round-leaved orchid, *Habenaria orbiculata*. Why only one, I wondered? And why only in that place?

I learned that round-leaved orchids like red maple groves. They also prefer rich, damp woods in the mountains. Pollinated by sphinx moths, a single pollination will fertilize hundreds of thousands, even millions of microscopically small light seeds carried by the wind. Apparently, one of those seeds had wafted to our Far Field.

A charming book published in 1904, *Bog-Trotting for Orchids,* by collector Grace Greylock Niles, recalls the days of abundant wild orchids. Niles herself concentrated on the Berkshires of northern Massachusetts and the southern Vermont valley of Pownal. Of the round-leaved orchid, then called the great round-leaved orchis, she wrote that its flowers were "strange, fantastic shapes, trimmed with spurs and hoods and capes. . . . The leaves were like large saucers, and of a beautiful silvery green underneath. The plant is always suggestive of the luxuriant tropics" (102, 172). Common names for the plant in her area were "shinplaster" and "heal-all" because the leaves were applied to bruised shins and were used as plasters for weak lungs. No doubt, between collectors such as Niles and herbalists, the round-leaved orchid quickly became rare.

Today the chief threat to round-leaved orchids is the white-tailed deer, as we discovered the following couple of years when the flower stalk was snipped off long before it bloomed. Finally, David fenced it and was greatly rewarded when he found it in full bloom with thirty-three blossoms last summer.

Today it was again in full bloom, glowing greenish-white in the dim forest light, its more than foot-tall stem swaying in the breeze, its two, nearly dinner-plate-sized, round, shining leaves hugging the ground. It wins my nomination as the most dramatically beautiful plant on the mountain.

In the evening the wind blew and it cooled a bit as I sat on the veranda waiting for summer to officially arrive. Chimney swifts coursed about high in the sky, chattering as they flew. Luz sat with me nursing Eva and we were companionably silent, since neither of us speaks the other's language very well, but we were able to enjoy the chimney swifts' acrobatics.

JUNE 21. A heavy shower left the mountain wet and cool again. A gray catbird sang in the first day of summer. Baby rabbits scampered off into the underbrush. The catalpa trees in First Field were in full flower. An ovenbird performed its distraction display along the trail.

As I walked down the road through the dripping woods, I thought, "Perfect red eft weather" and saw one sitting on the bridge in its glowing orange coat as if in answer to my thought. Like most of its kind, it had black eyes and small orange spots outlined in black on its back and head in a more or less random order of two rows.

The red eft is the land stage of the aquatic red-spotted newt. The larvae, after hatching from eggs in late April or early May, change into efts in late summer or early autumn and remain on land for three to seven years. Those that live on moist, forested mountains are the most brightly colored.

What I like about them is their fearlessness, as they walk boldly about in the forest during the daytime. Unlike most salamanders, they are not slippery so they can easily be picked up. They don't seem to mind parading up and down an arm or open palm. That was the first red eft I have seen here in several years, but they have not lost their charm for me.

Later I walked down the Dump Trail and was stopped dead in my tracks by a singing veery! The veery was in the laurel off the Short Circuit Trail and competed with a loudly singing red-eyed vireo in the dim woods' light. Then it flew down to the old dump area, all the while singing its evocative, downward-spiraling song. Only once have I ever heard a singing veery here and that was at the Far Field during migration many years ago. It had sung only a couple of bars before stopping, but this one today sang on and on, its echoing song following me as I headed home.

While we ate lunch inside, a doe brought her single fawn to graze in the backyard. It particularly enjoyed the leaves of the balm-of-Gilead branch that came down in a storm the other night. Then it started running at top speed, its ears pressed back, into the weeds above the old lilac bush and back down into the yard and halfway down the driveway. It made this circuit four times while the doe watched nervously. I've never seen a fawn that young running for what seemed to be the sheer joy of it.

JUNE 22. Another fledgling day. Along the Laurel Ridge Trail I watched a white-breasted nuthatch fledgling being fed by a parent. Except for a fresher look, it was a replica of the adult.

Up on the power line right-of-way, three mourning doves perched on the wires. After studying them through my binoculars, I was able to distinguish the parent from its offspring just by looking at their eyes.

All fledglings, I maintain, have a certain trusting, naive appearance, even if they do closely resemble their parents. On these juveniles I also noted the shorter tails and lack of a black spot behind their eyes, other giveaway field marks of mourning dove fledglings.

Next I spotted three blue jay fledglings in the top of a large oak tree beside the right-of-way. They all had gray backs instead of the blue of their parents, although they were unmistakably blue jays with blue tails and noisy, blue jay ways. The parents flew in as soon as they noticed me and the fledglings made loud, begging noises and held out their wings, evincing typical fledgling behavior.

Further along Laurel Ridge Trail, a large, dull brown bird with a thick bill that had light markings around it flew into a sapling. The bill gave it away. It was a rose-breasted grosbeak fledgling looking very much like its undistinguished mother. Only male rose-breasted grosbeaks sport the vivid rosy breasts that give the bird its name.

In the woods beside the Far Field I watched a black-capped chickadee fledgling being fed by a parent. Black-capped chickadee fledglings, like white-breasted nuthatches, are identical to their parents except for their "naive youngster" look and the "teeship" call they make as they follow their parents around for about ten days after fledging.

Finally, as I headed down the First Field Trail on my way home, two young birds fluttered up from the base of a laurel bush. They were nondescript brown birds with brown-spotted breasts. At first I thought they were ovenbirds, but when the scolding parents appeared, I knew that they were wood thrushes.

Eva, too, has been maturing. She is gaining strength and

weight rapidly and has become a little butterball. No longer an infant, but a bouncy baby, she coos to anyone who talks to her. She's aware of who and what goes on around her, and she eagerly pulls herself up to a standing position when I hold her on my lap facing me. Her favorite game, which she associates only with me, is "*so* big." As soon as I say those words, she holds my hands tightly and pulls herself up on her toes like a ballerina. This gesture seems so utterly feminine to me, in sharp contrast to our boys' rougher version of this game when they were babies. Of course, they pretend not to remember me playing such nonsense with them and groan every time Eva and I play. Only Eva and I are not heartily sick of hearing me say "*so* big."

JUNE 23. Another warm, humid day. An eastern phoebe sang at dawn, followed by an American robin. Undoubtedly their first batch has fledged and they are each gearing up for a second family.

The female eastern box turtle, who laid her eggs under the open grassy path at the Far Field back on June 17, was not so lucky. On that day she stood on the path, and as I approached, she did not pull in her head or legs. Knowing this was a favorite egg-laying spot for box turtles, I went off to look at the round-leaved orchid before circling back and again checking on her. She was still in the same place, still unmindful of my presence.

Today I found a dug-up area on the path a few feet from where I saw the female box turtle who refused to move. As I suspected, on that day she had been preparing to lay eggs, and now already her nest had been discovered and destroyed, probably by a raccoon. All that remained were the rubbery, torn-apart shells of two eggs.

Later, I walked the Black Gum and Rhododendron trails in the hollow. First a wood thrush, then a black-throated blue warbler sang along the way. An eastern wood pewee, ovenbird, worm-eating warbler, and several cedar waxwings called, and I watched a red-eyed vireo singing from tree to tree as it foraged. Moving as silently as I could through an Appalachian summer's deeply shadowed forest, I half-saw gray squirrels chasing and calling.

Descending the Rhododendron Trail, I found the first rhododendron shrub covered with pale pink blossoms. All the others I passed were white. I felt like an explorer who had stumbled onto great beauty and involuntarily I gasped at my first sight of a shrub filled with clustered blossoms, a single one of which would make a full, showy corsage.

The stand, high up in a steep, moss-covered side hollow, had been inaccessible to me before David and several of our hunter friends built a switchback trail last autumn, complete with stone steps, that winds finally down to the stream and road.

JUNE 24. I walked over to the Greenbrier Trail in the clear-cut area and found a festival of birds. First I watched a pair of cedar waxwings nest-building. One had a long twig in its beak. Then both gathered remnants of a tent caterpillar nest in their beaks. I walked within ten feet of the tent caterpillar nest and watched as one waxwing kept flying in and gathering the silk while the other came in to gather twigs from the tree holding the nest. Then both waxwings flew up into a small chestnut oak tree swathed in grapevines and built their nest in a tangled mass of grapevines about forty feet from the ground.

Further along the trail, a red-eyed vireo gathered insects from a low shrub. Its nest, crammed with youngsters, had been built in a red maple sapling about six feet from the ground.

A winter wren sang its haunting, echoing song far down a side hollow. A black-and-white warbler plucked insects from a tall red maple snag that had sprouted new branches up and down its trunk.

I pished quietly and first a female and later a male Kentucky warbler performed their distraction displays around me and then followed me a short distance scolding. Their scolding, in turn, brought a curious American redstart in for a close look. On Dogwood (formerly Clear-cut) Knoll, a male chestnut-sided warbler sang from the top of a red maple tree, followed by a yellow-breasted chat. Both birds nest in brushy clear-cuts and no doubt consider the hot, sunny knoll ideal habitat.

I returned along Ten Springs Trail. While Greenbrier Trail has mostly grown up in grass, hay-scented ferns, and black-berry, Ten Springs Trail has more bare patches in which huge common mullein, Pennsylvania smartweed, and rough-fruited cinquefoil, all wildflowers of waste places, grow. Baltimore orioles performed their distraction displays while eastern towhees protested my presence. These species also like open, brushy habitats and forest edges. Then a black-throated green warbler, who had flown in from the uncut forest below, landed at eye level on a shrub twelve feet away and sang its "trees, trees, murmuring trees" song.

In a wet area shaded by striped maples and a broken-off hickory tree overhung by wild grapevines, a black-capped chickadee family flew in close. Another pish enticed a male American redstart who snapped insects up in midair like a flycatcher. A foraging immature white-breasted nuthatch worked over a small, dead snag.

A scum of green algae covered a pool of water on Ten Springs Trail where we found wood frog eggs back in the spring. Today it was filled only with water striders gliding over the scum by rowing their elegantly long, thin, middle legs while trailing their equally long, thin hind legs. Deer and raccoon tracks surrounded the pool and tramped through it as well.

When I got home, Bruce pointed out a fantastic black and white moth, with white and gray spots outlined in black on its upper wings, metamorphosing on his rubber overshoes. It turned out to be an eyed tiger moth (*Ecpantheria deflora*) according to Holland, and the great leopard moth according to the *Golden Guide*. Both books agree that its larvae feed on plantain, which we have in abundance. The markings on its head do look like scary eyes and reminded me of the false eyes of eyed elater click beetles. Altogether it seemed more phantasmal than real.

JUNE 25. Two days ago I sat on the veranda in the afternoon and watched the eastern phoebe family at the top of the veranda column, the little ones bursting out of the nest, standing and flexing their wings and sometimes beating them in a rapid whir like pinwheels trying to get airborne. The parents occasionally landed in a nearby walnut tree with prey in their beaks. Some of the food looked like craneflies and once there was an orange and black butterfly, probably a Compton's tortoiseshell. The parents chipped before flying in as if trying to tempt the juveniles to fly. They also attempted to catch the young's fecal matter and sometimes even snatched it in midair, but often the young emitted it when the parents were absent so some of the mess started to accumulate at the base of the column.

This morning four phoebes were still in the nest while we ate breakfast on the veranda, but two fledged while I was inside before 8:00 A.M. The other two sat tight in the nest so I sat in the hall watching, determined to see them actually make their first flight.

A parent landed on the side of the nest and fluttered, then flew off. The youngsters preened their breast feathers and under their wings. They also occasionally poked and pushed at each other and watched the insects flying up close to the ceiling of the veranda. Then one youngster lay still while the other preened its back.

Again a parent landed and then fluttered just off the edge of the column before flying off, as if urging the young to follow. One youngster did stand up and flutter its wings briefly, but then both resumed their preening. After eight minutes a parent landed again, collected a fecal sac one of the birds emitted, and flew off with it.

Next, one of the nestlings sat up alertly, but both quickly settled back to preening, possibly a displacement activity for both of them and a means of delaying the inevitable. A parent again landed and poked at them and then flew off to perch on the nearby telephone wire.

Suddenly, light as air, one nestling fledged, flying perfectly over to its parent perched on the telephone wire and remaining balanced on that wire even after the parent flew off.

The last nestling perked up and preened constantly. Then it whirled its wings, stood on the edge of the column and faced into it before turning around again and settling back on the nest. Its just-fledged sibling, in the meantime, flew from the wire while the remaining nestling chirped and fluttered. I could hear one parent phoebe calling "fee-bee" in the distance.

Finally, with no parent in sight, the nestling abruptly launched itself out into space, flew to the other end of the veranda, and landed on a column post. From there it fluttered out to the same telephone wire and was gone by 8:45 A.M. So, despite what seemed to be elaborate delay tactics, the phoebe nestlings took only an hour to fledge.

JUNE 26. This is the second day of an oppressive heat wave so I was out by 7:54 A.M. to walk, clad in shorts and tank top, an outfit I wear only on the hottest of days. Even so, it was harder to breathe than usual. I felt almost as if I was swimming under water, and walking uphill was a struggle.

The chipmunks were busy despite the heat, running up and down trees chasing each other and foraging for food like squirrels. I sat in the Far Field woods, my back against the trunk of my favorite wild black cherry tree. A small, thin chipmunk moved slowly toward me, completely absorbed in looking and smelling for food beneath the leaf duff. Occasionally it found and ate some morsel and then sat up on its haunches to clean its face with its front paws. Finally, when it was only a couple of feet away, it saw me and rushed back to a fallen branch from which it called desultorily a few times. It quickly resumed foraging, this time moving away from me. It's amazing how often I can sit still in the woods in ordinary, even brightly colored clothes, and not be observed by wildlife.

In the warmth of early evening, as we ate dinner on the front porch, a Virginia ctenucha moth climbed over my fingers and arm, allowing everyone ample opportunity to admire its glossy black wings fringed with white, its electric-blue body, orange head, and feathery, black antennae. This common, day-flying moth feeds on grasses, irises, and sedges, all of which grow in our yard. Ranging from Labrador to Pennsylvania and west to Manitoba and Kansas, it has two broods during its season in the sun from May to July. Although its chumminess was probably due to my salty sweat, I am awed when a moth or butterfly lands on me, as if I've been briefly touched by the wings of an angel.

JUNE 27. I walked down the hollow road to pick black raspberries and was piped on my way by singing, calling birds; scarlet tanagers, Louisiana waterthrushes, wood thrushes, eastern wood pewees, and worm-eating warblers lent their voices to the chorus. The "babble" of humanity (the sounds of traffic), only reached my ears as I neared the base of the mountain. There I discovered a gray catbird on her untidy nest in a rosebush as I picked berries.

I hated to be out in the open picking, preferring to be hidden back in the woods like some wild animal. So when I was caught out in the open by a man in an old brown sedan who drove up to our gate, then turned around and headed along the edge of the railroad tracks, I picked hurriedly and nervously for a long time before relaxing and deciding he had gone on his way. Finally, with my berry bucket overflowing, I headed gratefully into the camouflaging greenery of the peaceful hollow and started the slow climb back up with my reddish-black jewels.

The usual array of red-spotted purple and great-spangled fritillary butterflies fluttered ahead of me. Then a striking white admiral flew up and away. It was a day for great-spangled fritillary romance. First two of them fluttered together in the road, one with its head near the other's rear. Three more mixed it up in the air, two of which took off together. Finally, I discovered two in flagrante delicto — the male holding on behind as the female carried him aloft. Then they landed in a tree where they stayed mated, looking like two leaves barely clinging to the bark. I also found one question mark and a gray hairstreak near the top of the road. It was truly a butterfly day.

JUNE 28. Although our neighbor Margaret has been dead for several years, she left us an unintentional gift that reminds us of her every June at this time. Many years ago she planted a catalpa (*Catalpa speciosa*) sapling near her home, a gift she had received as a schoolgirl on Arbor Day. As an adult she, like most people who have catalpa trees planted in their yard, did not appreciate the mess their long, pencil-shaped seed pods make when they split and release their winged, flattened, fringed seeds in early spring.

She was amazed when I told her more than a decade ago that I had carefully marked with white cloth each catalpa sapling I found growing in our First Field, offspring of her old tree, so that Bruce would not cut them down as he mowed that part of the field.

Catalpa trees are not native to Pennsylvania but have spread through cultivation after the southern species of catalpa, *Catalpa bignoniaceae* or Indian bean, was discovered in Alabama by British naturalist Mark Catesby around 1726. He promptly introduced the tree to England along with its Cherokee Indian name, catalpa.

For over a hundred years *Catalpa bignoniaceae,* which was native only to western Georgia, western Florida, Alabama, and eastern Mississippi, was considered the only catalpa species in North America. Then word came back from western settlers that an even larger catalpa tree grew in the Mississippi Valley from Arkansas and Tennessee north to Missouri and Illinois.

Dr. John Aston Warder, a founder of the American Forestry Association, described the new species in 1852 and named it *Catalpa speciosa.* Not only were its heart-shaped leaves four inches longer than the southern species, but its tallest specimens were one hundred feet tall instead of the sixty feet of *Catalpa bignoniaceae.* In addition, *Catalpa speciosa* could withstand colder weather, making it the more likely species to plant in northern states, although Pennsylvania does support both species.

Back in the beginning of the century, when many of our forests had been clear-cut, people worried about our wood supply. Because catalpa grows fast and is resistant to decay, it was cultivated for fence posts, railroad ties, and telegraph poles. It was also widely planted as a shade tree.

Its most glorious feature remains its showy, tubular, white flowers, their throats spotted with purple, that cover the tree in late June. For such a sight we are willing to put up with its messy seeds, to be grateful, in fact, that its method of dissemination has been successful enough to penetrate Margaret's woods and selectively reproduce itself in our field. Already its offspring are large enough to cast ample shade on a hot summer's day, and they make excellent blinds for wildlife watching because their huge leaves grow on branches close to the ground.

JUNE 29. Last week Mark and Luz decided to wash all of our windows including those in the basement. For years they had remained opaque with dirt. I had never felt it necessary to clean them because the windows are below ground level and look out only on window wells.

Once washed, however, they were so clean that you could see your reflection in them. So could a male eastern towhee. At 5:00 A.M. he began tapping on one of those windows directly below our bedroom. Except for occasional brief breaks to sing and forage, he continued his almost nonstop frenzy until evening, switching occasionally to other basement windows.

This afternoon I was driving friends back down the mountain after a visit. We had just watched a doe and her fawn running off from the stream, when ahead of me on the road I spotted a hen turkey walking along the crown.

"Look, a hen turkey," I exclaimed, proud to show off one of our more elusive residents to my wildlife-loving guests. "I wonder why she doesn't get off the road?"

And then we saw, and managed to count, ten reasons—ten small poults emerged from the weeds growing in the middle of the road. They were not more than a few days old, one of my guests said. The mother seemed unruffled by the truck driving slowly behind her and her brood.

What a procession we made. First, the hen turkey standing straight and tall, moving slowly, majestically—a queen—followed by her poults who dashed madly about, visible and then invisible as they zipped in and out of the weed cover. Finally, a large blue 1975 Dodge pickup with three gawking occupants driving at two miles per hour.

At last the hen turkey walked to the side of the road and stood waiting until the little ones stumbled up the low bank after her. We, in the meantime, recounted the poults to make certain they were all safe before we passed the little family.

JUNE 30. The towhee resumed his attack on the basement windows at 5:00 A.M. As if that were not bad enough, we also have a hyped-up gray catbird who insists on caroling every five minutes from 5:10 until 5:45 on the flat porch roof directly outside my bedroom window. Once I am thoroughly awake, he takes a well-earned break and then sings a long string of birdsong imitations, including snatches of wood thrush music, throughout the day.

At breakfast David reported that a black bear had invaded the guest house's small front porch at 3:00 A.M., rattling the almost-empty cat food pan. Then it uprooted and ate a flat of basil plants he had left outside to plant today. "It must have been an Italian bear," he commented. Although he couldn't see the bear, when he yelled to chase it away he heard it "woof." June is definitely bear month around here.

A hazy, humid morning and Laurel Ridge buzzed with gnats. The woods were silent as if the birds were already stunned by the heat. Sapsucker Ridge, as usual, was gnat-free and breezy and the birds sang, particularly rose-breasted grosbeaks, ovenbirds, red-eyed vireos, American redstarts, wood thrushes, scarlet tanagers, and eastern towhees.

A buck ran toward me full-tilt on Sapsucker Ridge Trail just as a red-eyed vireo landed on a shrub beside me, snatched up a moth, and flew off. The buck finally stopped one hundred feet away, peered intently at me, then slowly walked off the trail, disappearing into the woods as I stood still watching.

Late in the morning I stood and watched the tapping towhee as he jumped and tapped several times at each of the three window panes, moving methodically back and forth. Often he would launch himself from the edge of the window well to give himself more momentum as he fought what he thought was a rival looking back at him. I counted forty attacks per minute, which only stopped momentarily if someone came too near.

In the evening friends from the valley brought up a male fawn whose mother had been killed on the highway four days ago. They wanted to release him here where he would be safe from the same fate. He was still small and spotted, and he licked everyone in a friendly manner even though our friends said no one had fed him. He was especially fond of blond little Ariane and she of him, but since her father had explained that nature must take its course, she bravely waved goodbye and climbed back into the truck. The fawn posed for many photographs and sidled up to all of us including Eva and Luz, who were amazed to see such a creature. We ignored him and he finally wandered up the mowed trail toward the power line right-of-way.

Every 2.7 years we have two full moons in one month, the second of which is called a "blue moon." Tonight the blue moon shone brightly and fireflies flickered in the heat of June's final hours.

July

So you walk the roads and fields. The bees hum. The hot air
shimmers. Grass heads ripen. Summer possesses the land. And
you can smell July, honey-sweet, on every breath of air.

Hal Borland, *Twelve Moons of the Year*

JULY 1. Today I walked the Black Gum Trail in search of nesting birds. It was breezy, clear, and a cool sixty-five degrees. On this day the spent blossoms of mountain laurel littered the trail. A few tree-sized rhododendron bushes were covered with clumps of white flowers and they buzzed with fat bumblebees.

I counted fourteen species of birds along the trail. With the exception of a drumming pileated woodpecker, they were all migrants. Most were south-of-the-border migrants who prefer to nest in large tracts of mature woods. Red-eyed vireos, ovenbirds, worm-eating warblers, scarlet tanagers, black-throated blue warblers, eastern wood pewees, wood thrushes, Acadian flycatchers, and eastern towhees sang as I walked along.

A blue-gray gnatcatcher, black-billed cuckoo, and rose-breasted grosbeak made one appearance each, probably because they are not usually deep woods inhabitants. Twice an ovenbird displayed, erecting its orange cap and scolding, and

58

twice a worm-eating warbler displayed. The latter was by far the most dramatic.

First she came flitting close to me, scolding from the laurel shrubs. Then, as I moved toward her, she flew to the ground, scuttling low through the underbrush, shaking her wings, and constantly "chipping." Sometimes she stopped to snap up insects, and then she would resume her distraction display.

For a short time I sat watching her, and she came within three feet of me, still running and shaking her wings. Apparently her nest, as with the last displaying worm-eating warbler I encountered, was nearby, but although I searched, I again found nothing. That was not surprising, because their nests are well-hidden on the ground beneath a drift of leaves.

Worm-eating warblers are more often heard than seen. Their song is a dry buzzing similar to that of a chipping sparrow's. Both sexes are distinguished by their black-striped, buffy-colored heads on otherwise dark olive bodies. Because they skulk in heavy underbrush, particularly laurel thickets, I usually only hear their songs when they first arrive here in early May.

In addition to the two different worm-eating warblers on the trail, two more of them had, similarly, performed distraction displays in well-separated areas along Laurel Ridge Trail several days earlier. The fact that I'd seen so many in a few days seemed to indicate an increasing population of the bird on our mountain.

There also appears to be an upsurge of ovenbirds and wood thrushes, far more than I can remember seeing or hearing here since the midseventies. In fact, I thought of renaming the trail the Wood Thrush Trail, at least during the spring and summer months. All the while I walked the Black Gum Trail I was never out of earshot of at least one singing wood thrush.

How wonderful it was to be passed on, so to speak, from wood thrush chorister to wood thrush chorister as I walked. I remembered back several years earlier, when the neighboring landowner, the logger who had bought Margaret's property, called to tell us that we had "a fortune in trees" and urged us to consider cutting them. He had subsequently clear-cut his side of the hollow, while we staunchly maintained our belief in the value of large, mature forests.

We could still see, along the Black Gum Trail, remnants of the old pine trees that had been cut a hundred years before. And the many deep pits in the forest, as well as the moss-covered mounds—remnants of massive root balls—hinted at the size of the original forest trees that had fallen long before the first clear-cutting of the mountain for the charcoal industry in 1813.

We harbor the dream that if we let the forest alone, some day it may revert to a semblance of its former glory. In the meantime, we know we are providing valuable habitat for the wildlife that does not thrive in small forest openings, clear-cuts, or young forests. We see our "fortune" in an unlogged woodland where the wounds of last century's clear-cuts have mostly healed.

We told the logger that we already have a fortune—a fortune in songbirds and solitude, peace and beauty—a legacy we can pass on to future generations.

The newly released fawn was in the yard and on the veranda off and on all day. Once I saw a pair of ears at the kitchen window, and later he stepped into the dining room when Luz and Eva were stepping out. Luz managed to shoo him outside. Although he is appealing, almost as appealing as large-eyed Eva, we know that a tame buck, when he matures, will be dangerous. For that reason we are keeping our distance and giving him the chance to revert totally to the wild again.

JULY 2. A gray, drizzly day and I chose to walk down the hollow road beside our small stream. A pile of sleeping raccoons lay draped like a fur stole at the top of an enormous, broken-off oak tree that stands as a fifteen-foot sentinel beside the stream. While I watched from the road, trying to sort out their numbers, a deer snorted nearby, instantly alerting the snoozers. What had looked like two adults broke into four small raccoons who clambered down into the hollow snag, reacting not to me but to the deer's warning.

After a couple of minutes, two of the raccoons emerged from the snag. One instantly lay down, its back to me, and resumed its nap. The other watched me intently for a minute or two and then partly retreated into the snag. Almost immediately it was pushed out again by the other two raccoons, one of whom also looked me over thoroughly before all three turned their backs and joined the other in a nap.

I eased to within twenty feet of the snag, determined to share a little time with the trusting, less than half-grown raccoons, beguiled, as many people have been, by their endearing face masks. Occasionally an ear twitched as they slumbered on. After a short wait, one youngster awoke and looked sharply at me for several minutes before again settling back down. This gave me a chance to swat at the horde of mosquitoes buzzing around my face.

More silent minutes passed before that same cautious raccoon again roused up and climbed back down into the den while the others still slept. I stood to stretch my cramped legs and quietly examined the snag from every angle; the raccoons never moved.

I then continued on my way, walking the Greenbrier Trail, where I found a procession of common mulleins in bloom. Had I been a medieval traveler at night, I could have lit my path with them because in those days they were valued as excellent torches. I also found the delicate, pink and yellow blossoms of dwarf corydalis blooming in the fertile ground at the bottom of an old, fallen, barkless tree and from its root clump.

As I started back along the Ten Springs Trail, it started to rain, but it only dripped and rarely reached me in the heavy understory. By the time I returned to the raccoon den, thunder rumbled, although only a few drops of rain fell. Two raccoons were still sleeping outside, but as I walked past they awoke and looked at me. I talked quietly to them and they seemed to listen before slowly moving into the shelter of the den just as the storm broke.

The fawn made only one appearance this morning so we are hoping that he is adjusting to his natural environment. Without a mother to provide instruction and milk, we wonder if he will survive.

JULY 3. Returning from the Tyrone Farmers' Market at 11:00 A.M., I was startled by a low-flying helicopter that hovered above our gate as I opened it. This evening, when Bruce came home from the university, he told us that while he was filling up the car with gas, he had spotted a newspaper headline indicating that an eleven-year-old girl was missing from Tyrone. So that explained the helicopter.

Then, as we were eating dinner in the kitchen, I glanced out the window and saw several beefy, purposeful-looking men striding up our driveway.

"Uh, oh," I said. "It looks like they're searching up here for the missing girl." A bloodhound, straining at the leash, led them across our lawn and around the side of the house overlooking the flat area.

Bruce went outside to talk to the men while Mark, David, Luz, and I trailed behind. Luz, protectively cradling Eva, was particularly upset at the sight of what, in her country, would be a menacing, perhaps even fatal confrontation with authority.

One man barked into his intercom, "Plummer's Hollow. We're up at Plummer's Hollow." Because of expected holiday visitors, we had left the gate open, so in less than ten minutes the place swarmed with police cars, trucks transporting more bloodhounds, and two ATVs driven by rescue workers recruited from the area to help the police and fire crews in their search. Since the evening of June 29, when the girl had first been reported missing by her frantic grandmother, they had been searching the town and the banks of Bald Eagle Creek and Little Juniata River for any trace of her. Yesterday morning the bloodhounds and their handlers had checked our mountainside above Interstate 99, and today they had followed along the river for seven miles to Bellwood. Tyrone firefighters had also gone door-to-door asking for information. So at first we assumed that they were searching for the girl.

Everyone was reluctant to tell us anything even though they were circling our home with bloodhounds, but Bruce, as always, remained friendly and helpful. Eventually, one of the searchers volunteered the information that he had gone to school with our oldest son Steve. That local connection seemed to give him the right to tell Bruce what was going on.

They were not searching for the girl, but for a male teenager, the last person seen talking to her before she disappeared. The name meant nothing to us, but we presumed he was a suspect even though no one would actually say it.

After aimless wandering over our grounds, the bloodhounds finally settled on Bruce's brand new dump truck parked on the barn bank. They had found what a bloodhound trainer described as a "scent pool" around the truck, which had been parked there for days except for today when Bruce had driven it to the university. Unless the missing teenager had walked the mile and a half up our road in the dark (the only time we would not have seen him), it seemed impossible that the bloodhounds were on the right track. Nevertheless, when they asked to search the barn and the shed, we readily agreed. As we expected, they found nothing. I suggested that a more likely spot for trespassers would be Margaret's abandoned house. Led by Bruce, the dogs, handlers, and searchers walked over there, but again they found nothing.

The last time a girl had been missing in Tyrone—five-year-old Kathy Shea back in 1965—we had not been living here. Many people had told us how they had searched the mountain for days. Not a trace of Kathy had ever been found. To this day it remains a mystery, but some folks still believe that her unmarked grave is somewhere on our mountain. After all, when a person is murdered, what better place to hide the evidence than the unseeing forest? It is, to most people, an alien place, inhabited only by wild creatures, and the fact that we choose to live here makes us suspect. Surely we are hiding something; if not the bodies of kidnapped little girls, perhaps a taste for the bottle or drugs or abuse. So we all sat on the veranda, looking as normal as possible, cooing over Eva and cooperating with the searchers.

Finally, they all retreated back down the mountain for the night and we retired to bed. But Luz, an impressionable young woman who has been in the United States for only a month and a half, was disturbed by the incident and spent a sleepless night rehashing the scene, in Spanish, with Mark who tried to reassure her.

JULY 4. I glide down the green aisles of summer, awaiting the unexpected. I sit in the green woods, absorbing the peace and mystery like a sponge, wringing it out later when life grows tedious.

In the dense shade, Indian pipes glow with unearthly intensity, lighting up dark spaces. *Monotropa uniflora,* the saprophytic flower of midsummer's shaded woods, means "once-turned" and "single-flowered," because at first its single white pipe dangles downward, but when it is pollinated the pipe turns skyward and the plant blackens.

Indian pipes live mostly on the decaying roots of other plants such as trees and are particularly abundant during wet summers. Several years ago, in 1988, not a single Indian pipe emerged the entire drought-ridden summer, but usually a few will bloom even during dry spells. Other names for Indian pipes include "ghost flower," "corpse plant," and "American iceplant," all references to its pale, white appearance and cool, clammy feel plus its tendency to turn black and ooze a clear gelatinous solution if it is picked. Medicinal uses of the plant as an eye wash led to the name "eyebright," and its perceived value during spasms, fainting, and nervous conditions produced the names "convulsionroot," "fitroot," and "convulsionweed." All in all, Indian pipe seems the best name for this uniquely shaped wildflower that looks more like a fungus than a plant.

The "corpse plant" reminded me of last night's search, and I urged Bruce to call Troy, a hunter friend, to find out if he knew the young man they had been searching for and if he had ever seen this person on our mountain. Troy did not know the suspect, but he did tell us that the newspaper had described the missing girl—Melody Curtis—as popular in her Croom-A-Coochee, Florida, school and community, where she lived with her mother. Five feet tall, weighing eighty-eight pounds, with shoulder-length, dirty blonde hair and a thin build, she had last been seen wearing blue and pink shorts, a blue top decorated with white flowers, and black shoes.

She had come to Tyrone to spend the summer with her grandmother because her mother was having a difficult pregnancy. She had been here only a few days and had spent much of her time playing in a sandbox with local children. Her mother had told reporters over the phone that, "She's a country bumpkin. She's a little country girl that doesn't know how slick people can be." She was a friendly girl even with strangers. Why hadn't her mother trained her differently? Why hadn't she warned her of the dangers females must always be aware of?

As a child, my mother had told me not to take rides with strangers. When I was in the third grade, walking home for lunch as five-year-old Kathy Shea had been doing when she disappeared forever, my mother's warning paid off. My friend Ruth, the top honor student in the class, was with me. A man stopped his car and offered us a ride. Ruth accepted and was ready to hop into his car.

"But Ruth," I protested, "my mother told me never to take a ride with a stranger," and I refused. Luckily, Ruth followed my lead, and the man drove off in a hurry. That same man—a known pedophile—was arrested the following day. It was a close call I never forgot. Whatever childhood innocence I may have had up to then was gone. If only Melody's mother had been as wise as my mother.

At dusk two wood thrushes sang outside my bedroom window, and I lay listening, willing myself to remember their otherworldly chorus on all the thrushless days of a temperate zone year. Would I appreciate the song as much if I heard it twelve months of the year instead of a scant three?

JULY 5. Still no word about Melody Curtis. So, as I took my morning walk, serenaded by birds and soothed by a wall of green, I wondered if I would find a body. Or is it hidden, buried somewhere on this mountain?

It was so humid that even the rocks on the trails sweated. I too dripped with sweat and was plagued by whining mosquitoes while picking a few blueberries on the power line right-of-way before moving hastily on.

At the Far Field woods a flock of noisy blue jays protested my presence, announcing to all wild creatures my silent watching beneath a cherry tree. Once they flew off, a doe and fawn bounded past without seeing me. Both a chipmunk and a gray squirrel emerged to forage nearby. A gentle breeze picked up, making the woods tolerable, even pleasant, and blowing away most of the insects. It was as if I sat in an island of cool calm, surrounded but untouched by heat, humidity, and buzzing black flies and mosquitoes.

Along the Far Field Trail, just before I started up the hill, I spotted a messy nest with shreds of grapevines hanging from it, six-and-a-half feet high in a striped maple sapling. It was an eastern towhee nest containing nestlings. The female was agitated and flew close to me as I tried to reach up into it to verify hatched young. Other towhees called from every direction. According to scientific observers, towhee nests are never more than two to five feet from the ground, and most are on the ground. The higher nests are always second nestings as this one probably is. The habitat also was unusual— the black cherry woods with no shrubby understory, the nest perfectly obvious. Later I read in Arthur Cleveland Bent's *Life Histories of North American Cardinals, Grosbeaks, Buntings, Towhees, Finches, Sparrows, and Allies* that one nest in Grand Rapids, Michigan, was eight feet above the ground, and a Minnesota record set back in 1932 in a matted grapevine was eleven feet, four inches from the ground. The highest record was from Jackson County, Indiana, in 1952—seventeen feet, five inches—and was placed in a brushy tangle where the tops of two small shagbark hickory saplings and a vine of wild grape were interlaced. So, while my find was unusual, it was not record-breaking.

Our tapping towhee, whose nest I have not found, is still jumping and tapping at all three basement windows from dawn until dusk, interspersing his attacks with calls and songs from the back porch roof, the slippery elm tree, the small black walnut tree, the large black locust tree, and the herb garden juniper bush, defending what appears to be a half-acre territory that stretches from our backyard, around the side of the house, and includes the brushy slope below. He continues to look as fresh and vigorous as the day he began. Even the heat wave does not deter him.

In the afternoon I drove downtown. On my way down the

mountain, I asked our six-foot, four-inch son, Steve, who is visiting, to climb out on to the truck bed and retrieve the Acadian flycatcher nest for me, since, according to my calculations, based on when I had first discovered the nest back on June 12, the little family, had there been any, would have fledged. To my surprise, Steve discovered two fluffy young still in the nest as the distressed mother called in the background. So, of course, we left the little family alone.

JULY 6. Melody Curtis has still not been found despite massive searches. Yesterday 150 citizens from all over the area were divided into three teams and searched three designated hot spots—places where "the bloodhounds had gone bonkers," as one person put it, during earlier searches, or where she had last been seen. Meanwhile, I sat in the breezy, green woods near the Far Field, feeling safe as I always do on our mountain, and absorbed the peace of the shadowy green forest—a haven of rest and relaxation for me. There I watched spotted, twin fawns foraging in the Far Field.

As I resumed my walk along Sapsucker Ridge Trail, I glimpsed a black bear off in the woods. Unfortunately it caught my scent and bounded up the ridge top. Then it paused for a few seconds, enough time for me to admire it through my binoculars, before it ran out of sight.

A brightly colored female eastern box turtle plodded along the trail and hissed when I picked her up for a closer look. According to environmentalists, the pet trade is scooping up box turtles by the tens of thousands and selling them here and in Europe. Most of them die en route or after a year of captivity. Kids are paid a quarter per turtle to collect them, decimating populations on Long Island. What a pity if we wipe out this most common of turtles to put money in the pockets of the sellers and put wild animal pets unable to adapt to captivity in the hands of those who profess to love animals.

My brother Gary and his family drove up our road in

midafternoon and noticed the tire tracks of a vehicle that had driven around our gate. At the forks he encountered five very tense FBI agents who, mistaking him for the landowner, ordered him to keep the lock off the gate. They were searching Margaret's old house again because of a tip they had received. According to my brother-in-law, Bob, who works in a local factory, several of his fellow employees suspect that Melody, dead or alive, is up here.

Later, after the agents were gone, Mark and David went over to Margaret's house and found that the agents had smashed a lock to get into the house. Why hadn't they asked us, the owners of the property and house, to unlock our gate and the house? What right had they to come here without our permission? Jackbooted thugs, indeed! We swallowed our pride and ignored the incident, knowing that feelings were running high in a town that still remembered the horror of the unsolved Kathy Shea disappearance.

JULY 7. I have been reading and pondering Thomas Berry's elegiac *The Dream of the Earth.* As a nature writer, I feel increasingly out of sync with the rest of humanity. *Nature writer,* like *nature lover,* has become a derogatory term in our increasingly use-oriented, problem-solving society. The technicians have even taken over what used to be primarily nature-oriented magazines. Environmental articles by technical writers and journalists are crowding out nature writing. Instead of trying to create a world of nature appreciators, we are pandering more and more to what we are trying to change, an ego-ridden society interested only in nature for its practical value to people. We must save the rain forest, not because of its miraculous interrelatedness, its biodiversity, its beauty, its mystery, but because it may hold the cure for cancer and other deadly human diseases. We must stop polluting the oceans, not because of the sentient creatures being wiped out as a result of our greed, but because of the food potential for humans that we are destroying. We must clean up the air, not because it is killing trees and the very earth itself, but because it is hazardous to human health.

Something more is needed. As Thomas Berry writes, "Without a fascination with the grandeur of the North American continent, the energy needed for its preservation will never be developed. Something more than the utilitarian aspect of fresh water must be evoked if we are ever to have water with the purity required for our survival. There must be a mystique of the rain if we are ever to restore the purity of rainfall. This evocation of a mystique is the role that is fulfilled by the poets and natural history essayists. . . . In every country . . . a mystique of the land is needed to counter the industrial mystique" (32–33).

About the extinction of species Berry says, "To wantonly destroy a living species is to silence forever a *divine* voice" (46). I feel the same way, but few others seem to agree. Anything for profits. Why worry about a red-cockaded woodpecker, for instance. What does it do for humanity? No cancer cure there. It is merely a unique creature, one of millions that many people are willing to eliminate if it threatens jobs or private property rights. In order to save any endangered species, the government, or nongovernment organizations such as the Nature Conservancy, must bribe landowners with money or tax advantages or in some other way make it palatable for people to protect species. To merely protect it for itself is considered sheer craziness—caring about nature more than people.

Are just a few of us born to love the earth and all its diversity and the rest to use it only for their own purposes? Are nature lovers a dying breed, anachronisms in a practical world, or were they never represented in large numbers but were just a few cranks over the ages whom people ignored when profits were involved? I tend to think that nature lovers have always been a small minority of voices, set here to praise the earth, to keep alive the appreciative spirit and the old earth worship dismissed as pagan, and therefore evil, by later religious minds—those minds bent, as Berry says, on salvation, on earth as a vale of tears, on winning a better life somewhere else.

There *is* nowhere else, as Berry, a Roman Catholic priest, tells us. This is what we were given, this small globe spinning alone in the universe with its gift of verdant life. No other earth like it seems to be out there in the immensity of space. Yet, instead of feeling reverence for such a place, we milk it beyond its capacity to produce and little care that we will leave a greatly impoverished world to our children and their children.

Berry's solution is for humanity to give up its anthropocentrism and replace it with biocentrism—focusing on nature instead of humans. It sounds like a good idea but is probably unworkable given our species' self-centeredness. I'm more in favor of a deus ex machina, a Second Coming, a prophet able to persuade humanity of its wrong turning. Instead we will get more stupid and venal politicians. Visionaries are not wanted.

I took an evening walk, enveloped in heat, humidity, and a cloud of insects. Still, I grazed and gathered blueberries that have ripened along Laurel Ridge Trail until the sun set. Afterward, I gradually cooled off as I walked along the shaded paths, flushing a large, indeterminate fledgling and watching a doe emerge noisily on the trail ten feet ahead of me and then freak out, racing off in a frenzy of snorts as if to excuse herself for not having seen me sooner.

Best of all was reaching the Far Field and being serenaded by a pair of wood thrushes, their songs emanating from the dark woods like spirits.

I walked home, piped across the power line right-of-way by at least three more wood thrushes singing from the edges of the woods. Long after I left the woods, my ears rang with their tremulous echoes and vibratos. What a silent spring and summer it would be if no wood thrushes sang.

Outside in the misty dusk, the fireflies rose from the grass like sparkling phantoms. This summer, as always, I am mesmerized by fireflies and cannot get enough of watching them in the shadows—flashing pinpoints of light penetrating the dark night.

JULY 8. Today was a butterfly day because Bruce's oldest brother Bob was visiting us. At nearly sixty years of age, he has recently developed an interest in butterflies. Eating his lunch on his company's weedy grounds in northern New Jersey, he was fascinated by the butterflies he saw. So he armed himself with a large assortment of butterfly books and even purchased special, close-focus binoculars for observing them better.

In such an environment he sees mostly cabbage butterflies, one of our most common and widespread species that feeds on members of the mustard family and thrives in weedy habitats. Bob admires them for their industriousness and persistence because they are out foraging even during cloudy, cool weather, unlike most butterfly species.

Several days ago in New Jersey he had seen and identified for the first time a painted lady, which he studied for a half-hour through his binoculars, memorizing its pattern. He is sharp-eyed, patient, and persistent and possesses a scientific mind. He welcomes what he calls the complete detachment of butterflies from any association with humans.

"They completely ignore us," he says approvingly.

He found it hard to accept the variety of butterflies we saw as we walked along, and he particularly admired the dime-a-dozen great-spangled fritillaries. I explained that their larval plant is violets, a woodland species that would not grow in the weedy New Jersey lot. Painted ladies, on the other hand, are a cosmopolitan species that feed on over one hundred plants including thistles, mallows, and legumes.

At the Far Field he found another painted lady, clouded sulphurs, and an American copper. I also showed him an exquisite, jewellike, shiny red and green dogbane beetle that he studied through his hand lens, having even more recently developed an interest in beetles.

Finally, walking down First Field, we stopped to admire common wood nymphs, a northern pearly eye, and a silver-spotted skipper, all common here and denizens of deciduous woodlands, but as exotic to Bob as tropical butterflies are to temperate zone visitors. I also noted that the first black-eyed Susans were in bloom, one of my favorite field flowers of midsummer. Although I pointed them out to Bob, he had eyes only for butterflies.

At noon Troy called to tell us that a hiker had found the remains of Melody under a brush pile near the factory reservoir on our mountain but across the river gap. This area is a popular place with teenagers, hunters, and hikers. She had probably been raped and then bludgeoned to death, as far as they could tell. Since the body had been there more than a day, decay had already set in, and they needed to examine her dental records before they positively identified her.

I could only imagine the horror this innocent girl had suffered before her death, a girl described as active in her Baptist Church in Florida, who had loved to paint, ride horseback, and rollerblade. However, as a newspaper reporter wrote in the local paper, "She liked people which most possibly led to her death." The agony of her grandmother must be terrible. As a new grandmother of a girl, after having had three sons, I can only hope that Eva will escape a similar fate. In the end, her grandmother's vigilance did not save Melody. She had been eager to return and eat the brownies her grandmother had promised her. "You know I'll be back for those, Nanny," were her last words. But she wasn't.

Luz was especially horrified by the outcome and couldn't stop talking about it. Who had murdered her and why? The locals think they know, and it is the same teenager the bloodhounds had been searching for here. No arrests have been made, and every family with young girls is especially nervous, including Troy who has a young daughter. How do we keep our daughter safe, he wondered. How indeed, when so many girls and women remain victims in a society that is concerned but helpless in the face of evil.

Nature, as usual, was my refuge from the often hostile and incomprehensible world of humanity. This evening Mark called me outside to document a new bird species for the mountain—a northern rough-winged swallow. I grabbed my binoculars and went out for a look.

The swallows were extremely cooperative. Five of them sat companionably on the telephone line with a song sparrow and a common yellowthroat as we approached and studied them through our binoculars. Carefully we noted their stocky bodies with brown backs, white breasts, and a wash of beige at their necks. Then they joined the chimney swifts and common nighthawks foraging for flying insects in the evening air.

Whatever had brought them to our ridge-and-valley province, mountaintop farm? According to the *Atlas of Breeding Birds in Pennsylvania* they are infrequent visitors to the region except near rivers and their tributaries. Probably they had strayed up from the Little Juniata River in the valley where they may have nested in one of the old belted kingfisher nests or perhaps in a bridge crevice, road cut, gravel pit, limestone rock overhang, or drainpipe near water, their other preferred nesting spots. Unlike most swallow species, they are not usually colonial nesters, and I wondered if they were a mated couple with their recently fledged offspring. The timing was certainly right.

JULY 9. By now the woodchuck population is bursting at the seams. They graze on our lawns, our flowers, and our weeds. Except for the volumes that have been written about Groundhog Day, woodchucks have not been a popular subject with nature writers, journalists, or biologists. I must admit they have been my least-favorite wild creatures too, especially during the years when we had a large vegetable garden and no dog. No matter how deeply we buried our nine-foot-high garden fence and weighted it down with rocks, woodchucks always managed to dig under it. One spring a single woodchuck ate fifty broccoli and cauliflower plants in half an hour.

Now that we buy our vegetables at the local farmers' market we are able to appreciate the hordes of woodchucks who live everywhere on our mountain—in the deep woods of the hollow, the dry oak forest on both Sapsucker and Laurel ridges, the First and Far fields, and the several mountaintop thickets. Furthermore, at least five live in the vicinity of our house—under our front porch, below the back porch in the grape tangle, beside the garage, next to the road drain, and under the guest house.

I've found them outside our back door investigating the doormat, tearing across our veranda while I sat nearby, and parading over the tiny guest house front porch. They graze on our roughly shorn lawns and even eat the invasive crown vetch we foolishly planted on the steep back slope shortly after we moved here. Like white-tailed deer, woodchucks eat a wide variety of both cultivated and wild plants, but they also occasionally relish grasshoppers, snails, June beetles, and other invertebrates.

Before Europeans settled America, a much sparser population of woodchucks lived in the woods. Not only was it harder for them to make a living in such a habitat, it was difficult to escape their major predators—black bears, mountain lions, wolves, and fishers. Then settlers cut down the forests, eliminated the large predators, and planted succulent crops of alfalfa, clover, and other woodchuck-friendly foods. The living was (and is) easy except for the occasional woodchuck hunter, car, or smaller predators such as dogs, foxes, minks, weasels,

large hawks, and owls. However, woodchucks fight so fierce-
ly when they are cornered that such predators often retreat
before making a kill.

Researcher Robert Snyder has also discovered that woodchucks are susceptible to many of the same diseases as humans are—hepatitis, liver cancer, arteriosclerosis, heart attacks, strokes, even high blood pressure, so they have become
popular drug-testing laboratory animals. Nevertheless, there
is still one woodchuck for every five to ten acres in the Northeast, while the all-time-high woodchuck population explosion occurred at Letterkenny Ordnance Depot near Chambersburg, Pennsylvania, back in the 1950s, when Snyder and
others estimated that nine thousand woodchucks lived on ten
thousand acres.

A woodchuck's year begins in March. First the males ap-
pear and wander from den to den in search of receptive females. Then, a couple of weeks later, the females unplug their
den holes so the males can consort with them. After mating
with one female, a male moves on to another. If a mating is
successful, thirty-two days later a female gives birth to between two and nine naked, blind youngsters no bigger than
an adult red-backed vole.

The young are born in their mother's nest chamber, a part
of her larger burrow system that can be as long as fifty feet
and as deep as twelve feet and that also contains separate hibernating and latrine chambers. Both the hibernating and
nest chambers are lined with dead leaves and grass.

Trying to observe woodchuck burrow life has been difficult
for biologists. Consequently, not much is known about their
underground life. Mostly they live alone, hence their scientific
name *Marmota monax,* which means "solitary marmot." The
female raises her young by herself, a process that takes two
months. At four weeks of age they open their eyes and are able
to forage near the burrow entrance. At five to six weeks they
are weaned, and two weeks later they are on their own.

That's when turf battles begin. We often watch them chasing and even fighting in late spring and early summer, but by now they are more interested in eating than fighting. Like gluttons they shove food into their mouths with jerky movements that remind me of a Charlie Chaplin movie.

By late September our woodchucks resemble obese shag rugs. Such eating is necessary, however, because they must increase their weight at least 30 percent before they move into their dens, plug all the entrances with dirt, curl up into a ball in their hibernaculum, and sleep the sleep of a true hibernator for four or more months, until the urge to reproduce arouses them from their slumber.

JULY 10. It has been an outstanding year for the tyrant flycatchers on the mountain. The woods still resound every morning and evening with the slow, drawling "pee-a-wee" calls of the eastern wood pewees, and the young eastern phoebes, as always, are the most common of our home and lawn birds.

The tyrant flycatchers make up the largest family of birds in the New World. Approximately three hundred and seventy-five species live from Canada to Tierra del Fuego, but only thirty breed north of Mexico. Here in the eastern United States we have sixteen species of what are, for the most part, look-alike birds sporting gray-brown backs and wings and white or yellow breasts. Many species are more easily distinguished by their distinctive calls than by their plain appearance.

The pewees and phoebes are prime examples of this. Both are grayish birds of medium size with light underparts, but the pewees do have, according to the books, "noticeable wing bars" and longer wings than phoebes, which, to my eye, gives them a more streamlined appearance. They also do not twitch their tails as phoebes do when they perch. All of that may be true, but for those of us with less than perfect eyesight, learning their calls, their habitat, and their nest-making preferences is an easier way to separate one from the other.

Because eastern phoebes migrate north from only as far as the southern United States and Mexico, they begin returning in mid-March, a full two months ahead of eastern wood pewees, who must return from northern South America and make a hazardous crossing over the Gulf of Mexico. Usually they do not arrive here until the middle of May, one of the last of our breeding migrants. When I hear their drawling song, I know that summer is almost here.

By then the phoebes' first nestlings are ready to fledge and they are well into their second courtship. They still utter their monotonous, low-pitched, two-syllable "fee-bee" song, but in mid-June, when pewees are in top vocal form, the phoebes are too busy keeping track of their burgeoning families to do much singing.

For the nest watcher, phoebes are more satisfying birds than pewees. Finding phoebe nests is easy because they prefer to build them under the eaves or on the shelves of human structures. Eastern wood pewees are much more devious. The female builds her nest on a dead, lichen-covered limb in the forest and camouflages the outside with lichens so that it looks as if it were a part of the limb. I have never found a pewee nest, but I did find a pewee family once. Apparently the two youngsters had just fledged because the parents made a great uproar when I walked past them.

I don't know how many eastern wood pewees the mountain supports each summer, but judging from the number of pewee calls I hear, I suspect a good many. I can be far more accurate with eastern phoebe estimates. This summer the guest house portico nest alone has sent nine young phoebes in two batches into the world. The garage ledge nest produced five and so did the veranda column nest and the outhouse nest. So, all in all, I have observed the fledging of twenty-four phoebes.

As for the other tyrant flycatchers we had here this year, I can only report on species. For the first time we have a breeding pair of eastern kingbirds. We frequently see them perching on our old garden fence or on the telephone line. We also have least flycatchers singing along the margin of woods across from our lawn and a small stream, and the newly discovered breeding Acadian flycatchers in the hollow.

Least and Acadian flycatchers are members of that confusing genus, *Empidonax*. In the eastern United States there are five *Empidonax* flycatchers—least, Acadian, willow, alder, and yellow-bellied—so similar in size and color that they can only be reliably separated by song and habitat. In migration, when they are often silent, it is almost impossible to identify them by species. This causes incredible frustration to bird watchers who label them "those confusing *Empidonax* flycatchers."

Least flycatchers, the smallest and grayest of the *Empidonax* genus, prefer open woodland habitats and emit their characteristic "chebec" calls at frequent intervals in late spring and early summer. While we hear and occasionally glimpse a least flycatcher, I have not been able to find any of their nests.

Certainly our easiest resident tyrant flycatcher to identify by both sight and call is the great-crested flycatcher. Its larger size, cinnamon-colored wings and tail, and yellow belly, combined with its loud "wheep" call, are unmistakable, or so I had always thought until today when I found a bird that had been trapped in our shed. After a little effort, I managed to catch it in my hand.

It was small with a yellow breast and it shrieked like a banshee. Because of its color, I thought it was a warbler, but when Mark saw it he identified it as a great-crested flycatcher. I couldn't believe it. It seemed so small, and its call was nothing like the familiar one I hear so often in the woods. But it did have a cinnamon-colored tail, and a bird in the hand, as Mark pointed out, is definitely smaller than it looks in the bush or through magnifying binoculars. In addition, when birds are upset they give distress cries that are different from their usual songs.

I released it then—content to have held a great-crested fly-catcher in my hand for a short time.

I was already dressed for my weekly trip into town when Mark summoned me to our silted-in well. As we watched, a star-nosed mole scrabbled about in its stone foundation holes above a pool of two-inch-deep water, jumped into the water, swam across and back by paddling with its long, spadelike forefeet, and then clambered into the foundation holes again. It repeated this same routine several times. All the while it used its twenty-two-pointed "star" nose and the long whiskers on the sides of its snout, eyes, ears, and forefeet to feel its way about.

I lay down on a towel Mark spread for me in a vain attempt to keep my clothes clean and braced myself against a log in the middle of the water so I could get a bird's-eye look at the agitated creature.

It continued to probe with its nose and the whiskers on its forefeet. Frequently it wedged its whole body into a hole, but its dark, scaly tail hung out and whipped about as if it, too, was being used to find an escape hole.

David, who had joined us in our wildlife watching, decided it was trapped in the well. He used my large cooking sieve as a scoop, and after many attempts, which were thwarted by the lightning-fast mole, he scooped it out of the water, dumped it on the lawn, and watched it dig its way into the ground in seconds. I was reminded of the concluding lines in Mary Oliver's poem "Moles" in which she describes them as "pushing and shoving with their stubborn muzzles against the whole earth, finding it delicious" (11).

The star-nosed mole (*Condylura cristata*) is nicknamed the "long-tailed mole" for its long, hairless, scaly tail, the "black mole" for its plush, black or dark gray, furry coat, and the "swamp mole" because it prefers to live in water-saturated soils. Its most distinguished feature is its prominent pink, piglike snout ringed with twenty-two fleshy tentacles called Eimer organs. Although the star-nosed mole has excellent hearing, it is almost blind, so its Eimer organs, along with those long, sensitive whiskers on the sides of its long snout, eyes, ears, and forefeet, are used to probe for and search out its prey.

Unlike other mole species in Pennsylvania (the hairy-tail and eastern moles), the star-nosed mole is gregarious and often lives in small colonies with others of its kind. Sharing tunnels and runways, it is active both day and night and all year long. These tunnels are usually built in or near marshy areas or streams and open directly into water because the star-nosed mole is semiaquatic, using its broad palms as oars and its tail as a rudder when it swims.

All the mole species dig both shallow and deep tunnels. The shallow tunnels produce long ridges above ground, the deeper tunnels up to ten-inch-diameter classic molehills. In the latter the star-nosed mole rests, raises its young, and forages during the winter beneath the frozen earth.

In early spring courtship and mating take place and after a forty-five day gestation period, the female bears three to seven young in a spherical nest composed of dead leaves, straw, and grasses. In a month they leave the nest and are themselves capable of breeding at ten months of age.

The star-nosed mole hunts stream bottoms in search of worms and the larvae of caddisflies, midges, and stoneflies. It also relishes crustaceans, mollusks, and small fish. In its tunnel system it hunts earthworms, grubs, and insects, consuming at least 50 percent of its body weight each day.

Not only is the type locality (the place where it was first collected) for the star-nosed mole in eastern Pennsylvania, where it was discovered sometime before 1758 when the great Swedish classifier, Linnaeus, officially named it *Sorex cristatus,* but the first star-nosed mole fossils were discovered at the new Paris sinkholes near Bedford in south central Pennsylvania. Those fossils are about eleven thousand years old, and those subsequently found in nearby states are 700,000 years old, so the star-nosed mole has been around a long time.

After I returned from town I discovered that it was a wonderful afternoon to meadow-walk, prompting me to spend some time wandering about First Field. I followed our uncut trail white with daisies and yarrow. Later I walked up to the far right corner of First Field in search of butterflyweed. This area is drier and less overgrown and so I had a magnificent view of eleven butterflyweed plants, the most, by far, that we have ever had here.

As I wandered among the brilliant orange wildflowers covered with feeding great-spangled fritillary butterflies, I spotted a small, white-flowered shrub that turned out to be New Jersey tea. Because it is a favorite deer food, we had never seen it before on our mountain, so we took its presence as evidence that our deer management plan, aided by twenty hunter friends, was working. The large number of butterflyweeds was further evidence of a reduced deer herd, according to wildflower enthusiasts I talked to.

JULY 11. A perfect day for my fifty-sixth birthday, so I spent much of it out of doors. A short walk in the morning through First Field soaked me to my hips. Over at Margaret's I found the first orange jewelweed in bloom, but it had been heavily browsed by deer.

In First Field I again admired the New Jersey tea shrub. Tradition claims that its leaves were used as a tea substitute during the American Revolution, hence its common name. Another common name is "redroot" because of its large, deep-red roots.

On an early afternoon walk I followed Black Gum Trail to Pit Mound Trail, which I took down to the stream. A few birds sang—red-eyed vireo, eastern wood pewee, scarlet tanager, Acadian flycatcher, wood thrush, and white-breasted nuthatch. The woods were almost bugless, even near the stream, since the weather was dry and cool, so I took the opportunity to flip some rocks in search of salamanders and was quickly rewarded. Under three different rocks northern dusky salamanders quickly wriggled out of sight in the mud. Under another rock I found a large crayfish. I also saw a couple of inch-long young salamanders and a fourth northern dusky, this one with a yellow back, orange sides, and black markings.

The northern dusky is the quintessential small mountain stream salamander who often lives in a stream bank where the soil is damp. It seeks daytime shelter under rocks, logs, and leaves and never strays far from its place of birth where food—earthworms, snails, slugs, mites, spiders, and larvae—is plentiful. This five-inch-long, homebody salamander can be either gray or brown, and the pattern on its back varies with age. Usually it is identified as a dusky by eliminating all other possibilities and by looking for the definitive light streak extending from the corner of its eye to its jaw.

As I wandered beside the stream bed I also noticed a pair of fresh bear tracks in the mud and found where the bear had torn into a rotting stump, then climbed up the stream bank to the road. From there it crossed the road and headed up toward the clear-cut.

JULY 12. The hollow is studded with back cohosh this July, many more than we have ever seen before, their white flower spikes bent into contorted shapes that lean in every direction. I walked down the road this morning to look at them and found them covered with two species of black and orange longhorn beetles, some of whom were mating on the fluffy white stamens in the middle of the flower stalk. Although the cloying, sickly sweet odor of the plant almost caught in my throat and resembles that of milkweed, I could not agree with the old botanical books' claim that black cohosh has a fetid odor, like rotting flesh, and that therefore only carrion flies are attracted to it.

We have never found a carrion fly on black cohosh. In addition to many species of long-horned beetles, bees are also fond of the sweet blossoms, and we often discover both cuckoo bees and bumblebees making their rounds of the opened blossoms. After reading Stephen L. Buchmann and Gary Paul Nabhan's fascinating book *The Forgotten Pollinators,* I realize that very little still is known about who pollinates what in the natural world, so our observations of black cohosh pollinators are probably as valid as those of the old botanists. Most plants that survive in good numbers have more than one pollinator species. Those that depend on only one are usually those plants that are endangered. They have, so to speak, put all their eggs in one basket, and if that basket is dropped, the plant too disappears.

The so-called fetid odor of black cohosh allowed botanists to bestow upon it the generic name *Cimicifuga,* meaning "to drive away the bugs." Its species name *racemosa,* from which we get the botanical term raceme, is Latin for "cluster" and refers to the way the white blossoms are clustered near the top of the stem. Alternate popular names include "bugbane" and "bugwort."

"Squawroot" referred to its use by the Indians in speeding up labor and treating menopause problems, and "rattletop" is a reference to its pods of loose seeds. Because of this imagined resemblance to the noise of a rattlesnake, Native Americans also used black cohosh to treat snakebites. The pioneers, always interested in herbal medicines, maintained that it helped those suffering from rheumatism, whooping cough, tuberculosis, and St. Vitus' dance. Lately it has indeed proved helpful for female problems and is available even in drugstores, so the Native Americans were right on target when they used it for menopause complications.

Why the unimaginative name *black cohosh? Cohosh* comes

from the Algonquin word *co-os,* meaning "pine tree," a reference to the plant's showy flower spikes. A more beautiful,
imaginative name, also referring to its flower, is "fairy candles." Not only does "candles" describe the shape of the blossoms, but "fairy" bestows on it an added mystery appropriate
to flowers that seem to glow with an inner light in the darkness of a leaf-enshrouded wood.

In the evening as we sat around the kitchen table eating
dinner and talking with Steve and his wife, Karylee, who
were still visiting, Steve suddenly stopped in midsentence to
say, "Look what's coming," and pointed excitedly at the driveway. A big black bear, probably the power pole bear, was ambling down the road. We watched as he rounded the curve
and passed the barnyard, still on the road. Then we ran to the
front porch, Bruce snapping pictures with his camera as the
bear kept moving at the same speed. We tried yelling at him
to get him to stop and look up, but he remained wonderfully
aloof, maintaining his same steady pace past the guest house,
over the road grate, and out of sight down the hollow road.

Once again our charismatic megafauna had shown itself to
a daughter-in-law. This time it was Karylee's first bear, despite
a childhood spent in Alaska and Oregon.

JULY 13. A rhododendron shrub to the left of Guesthouse Trail was white with blossoms, the best single flowering shrub I've seen anywhere this year, including the huge
rhododendrons at the old growth forests of Alan Seeger and
Detweiler Run natural areas in Rothrock State Forest that we
visited early in the month.

Wood thrushes sang this morning. So did hooded warblers, scarlet tanagers, and red-eyed vireos. An ovenbird performed its distraction display along Laurel Ridge Trail, using
what ornithologists call the "rodent run" or "rat trick," according to Alexander Skutch in his book *The Minds of Birds.*
As he describes it, "alighting in front of an intruder, a parent

bird runs ahead of it with foreparts depressed in a hunched posture. With its tail depressed, the bird's trailing, quivering wings simulate the rapidly moving hind legs of a small rodent. Often, too, the bird's fluffed-out feathers resemble fur, and it may even squeal like a mouse" (99).

Along Sapsucker Ridge Trail I encountered a mammal we had previously only seen dead on our property—a southern red-backed vole. It was foraging in the leaf duff in our wild black cherry woods. At first I thought this lovely creature, with its distinguishing broad, reddish band running from forehead to rump, was suffering from brain parasites like a deer mouse we had found here many years before. Such an infection causes an animal to lose all caution and to circle as it moves along.

This vole nosed under the leaves and ate, then circled three to four times and shook its head before moving a couple of inches to its next feeding spot. As I watched, standing directly over it, it increased its circling to sixteen revolutions before each eating bout. Later I learned that it might have been my close attention and not disease that initiated the vole's strange behavior. Mammalogist Joseph Merritt says in the *Guide to the Mammals of Pennsylvania* that "when disturbed, the southern red-backed vole may exhibit 'waltzing,' a condition in which an animal makes rapid, circling movements from left to right and jerks its head" (193). How marvelous to have witnessed a waltzing vole!

The remains of Melody Curtis were buried in Florida today. At the same time a memorial service for her was held in Tyrone. Four hundred people attended as a local minister with a fine tenor voice sang "Amazing Grace" and "Jesus Loves Me," and other ministers tried to explain God's grace to humanity despite what seems like inexplicable horrors performed on innocent children such as Melody. Perhaps the attendees derived the most comfort from the flowering plum tree, donated by a local greenhouse, that was planted in her

memory on a grassy spot near the townhouse where Melody
last played with children in the sandbox.

JULY 14. It's a little too late to don the cloak of invisibility this summer. However, had I lived in rural England before
the nineteenth century, I might have gone out on St. John's
Eve (June 24) in search of fern seed, specifically those of
bracken. I would also have carried along twelve pewter plates.
Under the first bracken I could find, I would have stacked the
plates and waited until midnight. At that time, it was believed, the invisible fern seeds would pass through the first
eleven plates and land on the twelfth.

The twelfth plate's seeds would confer magical powers on
me. I, too, would be invisible. Even better, I would be able to
understand the language of wild animals.

This was one of many ways people explained the reproduction of ferns, until pteridologists (people who study ferns)
discovered the true story. In many ways, the truth is even
more fascinating than the old legends.

Strangely enough, although ferns developed as the first
true vascular plants 300 million years ago and have true
stems, roots, and leaves, they produce neither flowers nor
seeds. Instead, the ferns we usually find in the woods are one
stage of a two-stage reproductive system.

On either the undersides of the green leafy fronds (such as
the marginal, spinulose, and evergreen wood ferns) or on
separate fertile stalks (such as those of the cinnamon, ostrich,
and sensitive ferns) are spore-bearing parts.

The marginal wood fern, for instance, has thousands of
fruitdots or sori on the undersides of its fertile leaflets, and
these contain many spore cases called sporangia. Each spo-
rangium has sixty-four spores, and on a dry, windy day when
the spores are ripe, the sporangia burst open and catapult as
many as fifty-two million spores into the air per plant.

Those spores, if they fall on moist ground, germinate after

two weeks, and each develops into a quarter-inch, thin, flat, heart-shaped structure known as a prothallium. This structure produces both sperm and egg cells, which unite when the weather is wet. In fourteen weeks a tiny new fern is growing from the prothallium.

So the first generation of the fern reproductive system—the leafy fern itself—is called the sporophyte generation, while the prothallium is known as the gametophyte generation. This has given rise to the rather burdensome term *alternation of generations* for the fern's reproduction process.

Once a fern species is established in an area, it has other means of spreading, and these are often quicker and more productive than the alternation of generations. The limestone-loving walking fern, for example, has elongated, triangular leaves with long, thin points. When those points touch the ground, new plants sprout from them. Another limestone lover, the bulblet fern, produces bulblets on the lower surface of its subleaflets or pinnules (the leaflike lobes into which the leaflets on most fern fronds are further subdivided). Those bulblets drop off and germinate into plants.

Most productive of all, though, are those species that spread through rhizomes—underground plant stems that produce plant shoots above ground and roots below. Most notable of these are the bracken and hay-scented ferns, both of which grow prolifically on our property, bracken in the woods and hay-scented fern in open, disturbed areas such as the power line right-of-way and the clear-cut.

Bracken is a worldwide species, ranging from New Zealand to just north of the Arctic Circle and growing on every continent. As such, it has more or less set the standard for fern legend and fact. Its genus name, *Pteridium,* comes from *pteris,* the Greek word for fern. Furthermore, it is the only fern genus with just one species, namely bracken.

Although it does produce fruitdots, they grow in narrow lines near the margins of its leaflets and are nearly hidden by the bent edges of its leaves, which is probably why the "cloak of invisibility" legend grew up around it. In addition, because of its hardy rhizomes, bracken rarely uses spores for reproduction.

Bracken is common in Pennsylvania, but it is not our most common fern. The beautiful evergreen Christmas fern is supposed to be; but I'm willing to bet that hay-scented fern has or will shortly usurp its position.

Like bracken, hay-scented fern loves wet places and woods, and like bracken it spreads by rhizomes, taking over disturbed areas so quickly that little else can grow there.

Now known as *Dennestuedtia punctilobula* in scientific circles, it was once *Dicksonia pilosiuscula,* Thoreau's beloved Dicksonia, his favorite of all the ferns. To him, "essence of Dicksonia fern" was that of "an ancient and decayed herb garden . . . the very scent of it, if you have a decayed frond in your chamber, will take you far up country in a twinkling" (1519).

I must admit that when hay-scented fern began spreading on our power line right-of-way, I agreed with Thoreau. Essence of hay-scented fern, especially after it first uncurls its leaves in spring, is even sweeter smelling than new-mown hay. As the fern marched over every other living plant on the right-of-way, however, smothering not only tree seedlings but blueberry shrubs, black raspberry bushes, and pale corydalis, I liked it less.

Still, it provides a care-free ground cover that keeps the power company from cutting or spraying the right-of-way. And there is no denying the beauty of its yellowish-green, lacy fronds waving in summer breezes.

Then I began noticing other recently disturbed areas on the mountain succumbing to hay-scented ferns, especially those that had been logged. Ironically, when logs are dragged out of a forest, they turn up the soil and create favorable conditions for the spread of these ferns.

Even more ironic, the major tree species the loggers cut on

our mountain, red oak, apparently is unable to reseed underneath a blanket of hay-scented ferns. Why this is so and why the ferns are so deadly to other plants is still the subject of intense research.

One researcher, Tracy Hippensteel at Penn State, studied a three-acre plot in our area that had been clear-cut seven years previously and had grown up into hay-scented ferns. First she discovered that the fern fronds absorbed most of the red and blue wavelengths used in photosynthesis, allowing only the far-red waves, which are unusable in growth, to pass through to the ground beneath.

Next she planted white ash seedlings in areas containing from zero to one hundred percent of hay-scented ferns. By midsummer, those in the zero percentage area had grown twenty-one centimeters. Those growing wherever there were hay-scented ferns, regardless of how many, grew only thirteen centimeters.

So the intense, photosynthesis-absorbing ability of a bed of hay-scented ferns is not the only reason why other plants cannot grow in its area. Some researchers suspect that the fern is allelopathic, releasing toxic substances that suppress the growth of other plants. That theory has yet to be proven.

Whatever the reasons, and there are probably several, there is no doubt that the hay-scented fern has all the features needed to be successful in a rapidly changing natural world. It has two efficient methods of reproduction, it is difficult to eradicate naturally although there is an effective herbicide, and it can adapt to a wide variety of disturbed habitats.

Most of the ten thousand fern species worldwide are not as adaptable as hay-scented ferns or bracken, so when humanity alters their landscape, they are more likely to dwindle than to multiply. Pennsylvania, for instance, has approximately sixty fern species and, of those, ten are endangered. So far, I have found only sixteen fern species on our mountain—intermediate, marginal, and spinulose wood ferns; Christmas, hay-scented, cinnamon, royal, interrupted, lady, New York, rattlesnake, and sensitive ferns; and bracken, cut-leaved grape-fern, ebony spleenwort, and common polypody—none of which are rare. Except for the one royal fern in the Far Field thicket that refuses to increase, all have slowly spread during the quarter-century we have lived here, particularly the attractive rattlesnake fern. This, foresters tell me, is because white-tailed deer do not eat many ferns.

So ferns are spreading while those plants that flower and seed—trees, shrubs, and wildflowers—are dwindling because of an overabundance of white-tailed deer, heavy-handed forestry practices, and air pollution, among other insults. Once ferns were the forests of the Carboniferous age along with one-hundred-foot-tall club mosses and thirty-foot horse-tails. Long before flowering plants, mammals, birds, humans, and even dinosaurs, ferns lived in a moist, warm world of dragonflies with three-foot wingspans, giant spiders, scorpions, and amphibians.

Although our ferns have shrunk from their fifty-foot height, their shapes and reproductive systems have remained essentially unchanged, according to fossil remains found pressed between coal layers.

Such success over long periods of cataclysmic change on the earth is one of many reasons why both professional scientists and ordinary fern fanciers study ferns. Both continue to make new discoveries of fern species and varieties, methods of reproduction, habitat requirements, and distribution.

On a humid, muggy day like today, I go searching for ferns because, as the late Maurice Brooks wrote in his book *The Appalachians,* "Ferns are comfortable plants to live with, restful to the eye and a solace to the mind. They suggest coolness on a hot day, and water in a dry land" (198).

JULY 15. I set out on my morning walk in fog so thick that it blotted out vistas but greatly amplified the slightest sound. Despite the humid, soggy weather, the songs of the birds rang out cheerfully from the mist, and I identified, in quick succession, the songs of the eastern towhee, field sparrow, and common yellowthroat, and the distinctive calls of a red-winged blackbird and northern flicker.

Everything dripped. A sudden rainstorm in the trees ahead was actually a gray squirrel running along a tree branch, shaking off its heavy burden of water. I could follow the squirrel's progress by listening to the pattern of water dripping as the creature moved through the branches.

All nature appeared larger in the mist. The moisture beaded along every strand of spider web, revealing the hundreds per acre that are usually not noticeable on a sunny day. Many were intricate, lacy, orb webs of field spiders anchored between two weeds and glistening with minute droplets that outlined each delicately wrought strand. Others were dense white webs flung down flat on the field like fine linen handkerchiefs. In the woods one strand was strung across the trail and another draped over a branch, reminding me of a boy's string and stick fishing rod.

The light of endless dusk encouraged the songs of wood thrushes. Scarlet tanagers and red-eyed vireos also sang. Three American toads of varying sizes hopped out of my path in the fog. A red eft salamander wriggled along the forest floor. Indian pipes and mushrooms of every shape and color had newly erupted from the earth.

My hair gathered moisture as I walked along, encased in muffled silence, hearing only the drip of water from every leaf that moved and birdsong that continued to cut through the mist with sweet clarity.

JULY 16. Down below the back porch is salt-impregnated soil caused by a salt block we put there in ignorance years ago. Long after the block disappeared, the deer continued to paw at the ground, digging a deep hole in their quest for salt.

Today, as I walked down the stairs, I spotted, through a window, two fawns at the hole, pawing away in the dirt. After a while I located the doe in the grape tangle nearby. Then, another doe emerged from the woods followed by a prancing fawn. The two fawns at the hole froze, watching the pair, but the doe and her fawn stayed down in the flat area and soon disappeared from sight in the high weeds.

The two fawns pawed at the hole until their mother approached. One fawn moved away, but the other tried to paw with the doe. Each time the doe swiped at the fawn's back twice with her right front hoof, reminding me of a human mother slapping the fingers of a recalcitrant toddler. Both fawns finally took the hint and trotted down into the weedy flat area, leaving the doe alone to paw at the salty soil.

Then an eastern phoebe landed on a bare blackberry cane that hung over the doe. From its perch, the bird swooped down four times to catch flies off the doe's back, head, and rump in lightning movements so deft that the doe did not realize what was happening although each time after the fact she did look around.

Eventually she moved off and the phoebe flew away. I found it remarkable that the bird had the moxie to catch flies in such a way, an action of mutual benefit despite the doe's ignorance of the bird's help.

My friend Colette came to share my usual walk today. Even though she is more than eight decades old, she walked well and was eager to learn more—about ferns, about wildflowers, about butterflies, but especially about birds. She has been feeding them for years and often goes on bird walks and takes bird-watching vacations. Still, I taught her some new songs today, those of the field sparrow, Acadian flycatcher, red-eyed vireo, scarlet tanager, and eastern wood pewee.

Later, sitting on our front porch, which is elevated twenty feet above the ground and surrounded by trees, she had a wonderful time watching the birds, especially when she had the chance to see and study her very first eastern wood pewee. All that I take for granted was a gift to her. Caring about nature not only keeps her young at heart, but younger and trimmer in body than most of her contemporaries. But then most people who truly care about nature seem to be younger than their years. Concentrating on and appreciating something besides themselves and the human race in general seems to be the fountain of youth so many humans are seeking.

JULY 17. Butterflies, "caterpillars in wedding gowns" as one person so beautifully described them, are a delightful part of our summer, especially when the milkweed is in bloom. Milkweed, along with other so-called weeds such as thistle species, dame's rocket, black-eyed Susan, boneset, Joe Pye weed, aster species, and yarrow are the most important nectar sources for butterflies in the eastern United States.

Perhaps that is one reason we have such a large variety of butterfly species on our mountain—forty-five—because we have all those wildflowers in abundance. Looking over our butterfly list, I am charmed by the imagination of butterfly namers. We have the question mark and the comma, white admiral and red admiral, the northern cloudy wing and mottled dusky wing, the painted lady and the American painted lady. Among the showy swallowtails we have seen the pipevine, tiger, black zebra, and spicebush, although the tiger and spicebush are the common species while the pipevine and black zebra were only one-time sightings. Our butterflies range from the ubiquitous cabbage butterfly to the elusive mottled dusky wing.

Each butterfly is different in food preferences, migratory habits, personality, and even color patterns in the same species. The dotted skipper, for instance, is widespread but differs in coloration from individual to individual and from one geographic area to another. Some butterflies such as the American copper, northern cloudy wing, silver-spotted skip-

per, and common sooty wing are pugnacious, flying out from
perches and battering larger butterflies, birds, dogs, and even
butterfly collectors with their wings to defend their territory
or in search of receptive females. Others are peaceable creatures.

There are butterflies that migrate—monarchs, painted
ladies, buckeyes, purple wings, great southern whites, cloudless sulphurs—and others that never stray more than a few
hundred feet from their favorite food. For example, the Baltimore, as a larva, seldom wanders more than one hundred
yards from its only food plant, the turtlehead, even though in
its adult stage it takes nectar from other plants as well.

Then there are butterflies that form sleeping assemblies,
gathering in groups late in the afternoon and spending the
night together, probably for protection from predators. Both
spicebush and tiger swallowtails have been observed doing
this, although I have never seen them. I have, however, observed mud puddle clubs, swarms of butterflies gathered at a
mud puddle to obtain moisture and possibly salts, particularly the various sulphur butterflies.

Even courtship techniques vary among butterflies. Some
males have special scales on their wings called androconia that
emit a strong, distinctive scent to attract females. Often this
odor can be detected by humans. Some researchers claim that
male monarchs smell like especially potent wild roses. Other
butterfly species emit scents resembling chocolate cream,
lemon verbena, meadowsweet, heliotrope, sweet briar, san-
dalwood, and orris root.

One thing all butterflies do have in common is their development. First the females lay their eggs on the leaves of the
special plant that nourishes the larva. The eggs are light in
color when they are laid but darken before they hatch into
stage two, the larval or caterpillar stage. After five complete
skin sheddings, the caterpillar spins a support of silk and becomes a mummylike chrysalis. Finally, the chrysalis bursts

open and a full-grown butterfly emerges. The procedure never varies but the time element does. Here in the north many butterflies pass the winter in one of the four stages before completing their life cycles.

I feel privileged to have such a wide variety of species on our mountain, especially since butterflies are becoming scarce in many areas. Not only are they being poisoned by various pesticides, but their living space has been turned into super-highways, condominiums, monocultural farms, and other kinds of development.

"Where have the butterflies gone?" people frequently ask. Here on our mountain the butterflies are safe for the time being because we refuse to use pesticides, and we let the weeds grow, even the six-foot-high bull thistles considered pest species to be eradicated by most good-thinking citizens. But then they may have never seen a bull thistle covered with tiger swallowtails and great-spangled fritillaries on a day in mid-July as I did this morning.

JULY 18. Since we have lived on the mountain, First Field has become a meadow. A field is usually defined as "land appropriated to pasture or tillage," but a meadow is land that is "permanently covered with grass which is mown for hay." It also conjures up visions of butterflies dancing, birds singing, and wildflowers growing among the grasses.

To a naturalist, a wild meadow is an improvement over a cultivated field. It is a place to wander, as I did, this sunlit, breezy afternoon, absorbing the tableau of the natural world that surrounded me. Red-winged blackbirds called from sturdy clumps of goldenrod, common yellowthroats sang their "witchedy, witchedy" songs, and blue jays shrieked their warning cries from overhead.

I watched the barn swallows swooping and diving, seining the air for insects to carry back to their nestlings in the second story of our barn. In another part of the meadow, vigilant parent birds screamed at young American kestrels, already fledged from their power pole nest.

I waded through grasses that sometimes were shoulder high and other times came only up to my knees. Nevertheless, as they rippled in the wind, I felt as if I were seaborne instead of landlocked. Even the air reminded me of a fresh ocean breeze.

Often the sea of green was punctuated by the yellow of butter-and-eggs, common evening primroses, and St. John's wort. Ultimately I was drawn to the pale purple of a large patch of Canada thistles, presided over by hundreds of cabbage butterflies that twirled and spun in the sunlight, frequently dipping down to taste the delights of thistle nectar. Honeybees, bumblebees, and dozens of orange meadow fritillary and common sulphur butterflies joined them in the feast.

As I stood watching, I was reminded of how often "useless" weeds have provided visual treats for me. Later I took Bruce up to enjoy and photograph the remarkable scene. In our minds we cordoned off the thistle patch as a place to save the next time he mows the meadow, a job he performs just often enough to keep the meadow from reverting to forest.

Several years ago we also eliminated common milkweed from the mowing schedule and have been rewarded with a beautiful, sweet-scented sight every July. The honeybees, along with many species of colorful beetles and butterflies, find our spreading milkweed patches irresistible. During my walk the milkweed flowers were only starting to bloom, yet already the honeybees and great-spangled fritillaries fed on them.

Thorny shrubs such as blackberry and black raspberry are also ignored when we mow, not only because I like to pick berries but because they provide excellent nesting habitat for birds. In one thorny patch indigo buntings had hidden their nest, but the shrieking of two well-feathered nestlings gave the location away. Chipping sparrows and field sparrows also favored the patch although I didn't find any of their nests.

Eventually I sought the shaded edge of the meadow directly beneath Sapsucker Ridge. As I meandered along, a spotted, half-grown fawn suddenly rose from the sheltered grasses directly in front of me and ran off into the woods. A few minutes later a doe dashed across the meadow toward Laurel Ridge. I learned today that meadows not only dance with butterflies, glow with wildflowers, and reverberate with bird songs, but they also hide the small and not so small from inquisitive eyes.

I walked homeward, bathed in a peaceful aura that lasted the rest of the day, rejoicing that our workaday field had become a glamorous meadow.

JULY 19. Stupendous thunderstorms beginning at four this morning have turned our stream into a raging torrent and washed out sections of the road. Water streamed off the clear-cut area, now in its dangerous fifth year when the roots of the lumbered trees have rotted and lost their holding power. Because the loggers had cut all the trees along the water courses on what was formerly Margaret's land, those areas gushed with water that swept across the road, cutting deeply through the road gravel. The ditches on the mountain side of the road that Bruce had dug in the spring helped, but the road continued to drop away on the stream side where he hopes to erect a gabion wall next month.

Another section of the road bank had broken away in the first steep part near the bottom of the mountain where Bruce had pieced in locust logs in an effort to hold the road. This is also one of the major places in our hollow where small landslides frequently occur, so no vegetation survives on the road bank.

The reason this is a landslide area was determined back in the 1970s when Penn State geologists, using instruments called tilt meters, measured the up-and-down movements of the earth (somewhat like tides in the sea), along a line from Tyrone to Mount Union. This geologic feature, which they call a major lineament (comparable to a fault), has produced many smaller fault lines referred to as fracture traces and lineaments, several of which crisscross our hollow. One of the consequences of these fracture traces and lineaments is that the land is subject to sliding—a major reason why we opposed logging on the steep, unstable mountainsides on either side of the hollow. Not coincidentally, the places where the road bank continues to collapse are at the points where the fracture traces and lineaments cross the bottom of the hollow.

I drove down the road with Bruce this morning. We were both headed to the university for the day—he to his job at the library, I to do research. Mark joined us for the hour it took to help Bruce clear some of the road drains. Later, at noon, another fierce storm did more damage, which Mark and David tried to repair as it happened.

At the same time we were battling to save the road, there were floods all over western Pennsylvania from similar storms. Eleven counties were declared federal disaster areas, including our own, the second time for most of them in six months.

Surely this atypical July weather is another effect of global warming? For the first twenty years we lived here we had only a few winter emergencies and one hurricane. Since the early 1990s weather disasters have multiplied, one of the predicted outcomes of global warming. Bruce and David's continual road work barely helps in these emergencies. It's a good thing we now have the income to afford a secondhand bulldozer, a dump truck, and constant applications of gravel to try to keep at least even with the destruction.

JULY 20. This morning I walked the Ten Springs Trail. As I started down past the unlumbered section of woods, two broad-winged hawks started to call back and forth and one, a juvenile, landed in a dead tree nearby. I sat and watched it for several minutes as it watched me, fumbled about on the limbs, and called plaintively, opening its beak wide. This was the best look I'd ever had at a juvenile broad-winged, with its speckled brown upper breast, streaked face, underparts white halfway down beneath the tail and then dark with a slight notch, and dark brown back. The expression in its eyes denoted fear, confusion, and upset, and when it stepped onto another branch, it seemed awkward.

Red-eyed vireos continued to sing, unconcerned that a raptor called in their midst. Finally the hawk flew off toward the sound of the other calling bird and they continued calling back and forth. Walking on, I had a good view of both the juvenile and the adult. The adult broad-winged had some reddish-brown on the back of its head and reddish-brown streakings on its upper breast and shoulders. Otherwise, its lower breast and underparts were white, its wings were brown and white, and it had some gray on top of its head.

Ten Springs Trail, in the clear-cut areas, was already blazing hot. So I moved quickly into the shaded areas where the inevitable Pennsylvania smartweed and hay-scented ferns are taking over. The temperature difference between the shaded and sunny areas was at least ten degrees. A singing black-throated green warbler foraged in the top of a locust tree in the partially cut area and then flew back down into the uncut hollow area to sing. I frequently stopped to pick and eat the first ripe blackberries from canes that overhung the trail in places. Most were still green, however, and had been heavily browsed by deer who seem able to ignore the sharp thorns, indiscriminately eating leaves, canes, thorns, and unripe berries.

Finally, having had enough of heat and briars, I climbed back into the shaded, watered hollow, returning to a living, breathing, respirating earth.

JULY 21. Our mountain is awash in babies, youngsters, and teenagers, none of which are human, but, like human youth, they are full of uncertainties and demands.

At any time of the day there are spotted American robin youngsters hopping on the lawn with pieces of worms in their beaks. In the background I hear the constant calls of their parents who presumably are encouraging their offspring to eat the wriggly creatures they carry instead of parading around with them like human teenagers driving the family car for the first time.

Some of the youngsters make honest mistakes. The other morning Bruce summoned me to the garage.

"Look what's in the car," he said with a chuckle. An eastern phoebe fledgling sat quietly on the passenger's side of the car floor. Bruce had carefully closed the window on that side of the car the evening before because the garage phoebes' nest, with its second batch of nestlings, is on a ledge above it, but he had left the driver's side open. Somehow the fledgling had flown over the top of the car and into the open window where it had left a small white "package" on Bruce's seat before ending up on the floor. It was the package that had alerted him to the solemn youngster's presence. While its four siblings still in the nest craned their necks to watch, Bruce carefully picked up the fledgling and released it outside the garage. It flew off amid a chorus of cries from its parents who were perched on the electric wires.

The strangest episode occurred this evening when Bruce went out with the hand pruners to cut down the locust sprouts in First Field. He was dressed in brown and moved along quietly in a bent-over position. Soon he heard an intermittent whine that sounded almost like a mosquito in his ear. At first he ignored it, but the noise persisted. To his amazement, a spotted fawn stood up from the tall grass six feet in front of him, and, looking hopefully toward Bruce, resumed its whining.

"I'm not your mother," Bruce told it quietly, but the fawn refused to believe him and, blinking its long eyelashes, moved even closer. Bruce continued working as the fawn watched and whined. Twice he heard the fawn's real mother calling from the edge of the woods, but it took the youngster fully five minutes before it made up its mind and slowly trotted toward the waiting doe.

Eva, on the other hand, recognizes all of us, especially Luz who, like the fawn's mother, supplies bountiful breast milk, the only food Eva has had so far.

JULY 22. This morning I heard a noise in the living room chimney and carefully opened the woodstove doors, keeping the screen in place. Then the phone rang and after I hung up from a brief conversation, I once again heard a flapping coming from the living room. It was a chimney swift, still immaculate, unlike the bird Bruce pulled out of the stove several days ago who had been so thickly covered with ashes that it was unidentifiable. I had a long look at this one's roundish head, alert eyes, and long, tapered wings, and I carried it against my chest, speaking soothingly to it. I practically hypnotized it because when I opened my hand outside to release it, it merely lay there for at least half a minute before it finally flew off. I think we can add another breeding bird to our mountain list.

At last the tapping towhee is silent. Yesterday, twenty-three days after he had begun his assault on the basement windows, he tapped less vigorously and frequently. His mate has finally hatched her second brood, and he has had to assume his fatherly duties.

The female eastern towhee builds the nest by herself in three days, lays two to six eggs, and broods them for twelve to fourteen days, while the male busies himself singing and defending his territory. If the tapping male's mate spent three days nest-building, laid six eggs in six days, and then brooded them fourteen days, the total would have come to twenty-three days, exactly the time the male had spent attacking our basement windows.

Since I had never heard of such behavior by eastern towhees, I decided our tapper had been endowed with more testosterone than other male towhees. Then I discovered an account by F. W. Davis (573–74) of Massachusetts who had had a towhee tapper even more determined than ours.

"While his mate was incubating in June 1960, a male towhee discovered his reflection in the windows of a nearby house," he wrote. "From crack of dawn until dark he attacked his image with time out only to feed. He would flutter against a pane for a few seconds, take a few tentative but firm pecks at it, retreat, give a few 'drink-your-tea' calls, and then return to drive off the interloper. . . . He continued this behavior even after the eggs hatched. On his way to feed the young with a beakful of larvae he usually tarried long enough to make a few sallies. Ultimately he fought with—and smeared—every window in the house."

Poet Brendan Galvin also hosted a tapping towhee. In his "Poem of the Towhee," he writes: "This one has bunted the window all spring, baffled by glass."

First discovered and painted by artist-cartographer John White during a visit to the doomed Roanoke Island settlement in 1585–86, the eastern towhee (*Pipilo erythrophthalmus*) was, for a time, one-half of a continentwide species—the rufous-sided towhee. In 1995, however, the American Ornithologists' Union gave us two species instead of one. Drawing a line through the central great plains, they declared that east of the line the rufous-sided towhee was now the eastern towhee and west of the line it was the spotted towhee.

No matter what the scientists call it, the towhee knows its name, calling "tow-hee" or "che-wink" whenever it is alarmed, at all seasons of the year. The male's primary song, "drink-your-tea-ee-ee-ee-ee," is sung only during breeding.

Each male has his own repertoire of different song patterns. For instance, I often hear males that sing only "your-tea." They also vary in tone quality. Some are musical; others are buzzy. Frequently, males on adjacent territories countersing, each bird alternating his song with his neighbor's.

The eastern towhee is a satisfying bird because not only does it have easy-to-identify calls and songs, but an easy-to-identify body. One of its nicknames is "ground robin" because the male towhee exhibits the same black, brick red, and white color combination as the American robin. To my eyes, he is a handsomer bird. His belly is white, his sides robin-red, and his head, chest, back, and wings coal-black. His long, elegant tail is mostly black except for white corner patches that flash as he vigorously scratches in the underbrush, hence the "ground" of "ground robin" and his other nickname, "brush robin." The female is almost as striking, substituting a warm, reddish-brown where the male is black.

According to the *Atlas of Breeding Birds in Pennsylvania,* the eastern towhee is common in every county but Philadelphia. During the annual Breeding Bird Survey from 1966 to 1987, it was the eighteenth most common breeding species and the twenty-second most common species even though it declined 5.5 percent every year of the survey. This same decline has been noted across its range, but especially from New Jersey north to New England, varying from 5.6 percent in Maine to 13.3 percent in Vermont.

Although scientists classify the eastern towhee as a habitat generalist because it lives from sea level to upland forests, it does require brushy undergrowth and is partial to regenerating forests. Those forests must have a dense shrub and small tree understory and a thick accumulation of litter in which the eastern towhee scratches with both feet while searching for food. The eastern towhee, in other words, thrives in a messy, natural environment, especially old field thickets and later stages of second-growth forest. Such habitats are rapidly disappearing as we replace them with suburban sprawl, large expanses of sterile lawns, and intensively managed farmland. But our shrubby, seldom-cut home grounds had obviously attracted the tapping towhee and his mate.

The older male towhees are the first to return from Virginia, North and South Carolina, Georgia, and Florida where they have spent the winter, arriving a week ahead of the younger males and females. After remaining in small groups for a few days, they disperse, and each male forms his territory of between one-half to two acres by circling his chosen area and singing from perches ten to fifteen feet high or while he is foraging on the ground.

In the midst of such territorial disputes, the females return. They are chased by one or more males, and both sexes spread their tails to show off their white markings. They also warble back and forth and exchange frequent "tow-hees." Sometimes a male eastern towhee will carry and drop nesting material in front of his chosen female.

In Pennsylvania the eastern towhees are paired and begin nesting in late April or early May. Sometimes a male may occasionally visit the nesting female with food shortly before the eggs hatch in what ornithologists call "anticipatory food-bringing," but most males wait until the eggs hatch. Then these monogamous birds become model husbands and fathers, bringing food to the nestlings and sometimes to the brooding females as well. The male also guards the nest when the female goes off in search of food.

During the first few days, both parents feed their young by regurgitation, placing their bills into the gullets of their nestlings and pumping vigorously. Mostly the nestlings are fed insects, such as caterpillars, moths, bugs, grasshoppers, ant and fly pupae, beetles and beetle larvae, and spiders and spider eggs. As the nestlings mature they are also fed some fruits, most notably wintergreen berries, blueberries, and huckleberries. The nestling phase lasts nine to eleven days, and the fledgling phase between three and four weeks.

An eastern towhee generally survives from one to four

years, although one male in South Carolina reached the venerable age of twelve and another in New Jersey returned to the same woodland for six years. In fact, the male eastern towhee faithfully returns to his same breeding site at least 48 percent of the time, according to one study of a Pennsylvania woodlot. This means that chances are good that the tapping towhee will be back next summer.

JULY 23. Queen Anne's lace is in bloom in First Field. Although farmers call it "the devil's plague," those of us who love this showy wildflower prefer "Queen Anne's lace," "wild carrot," or "birds-nest."

Queen Anne's lace, like many of our favorite field flowers, is a green immigrant from Europe. The name "Queen Anne's lace" refers to Anne of Denmark, queen of England's James I, who was a talented lacemaker and wore dresses elaborately trimmed with lace.

The botanical name of Queen Anne's lace, *Daucus carota*, originally meant "orange" in both Greek and Roman, a reference to its root, which some botanists believe is the forerunner of our garden carrot, hence the name "wild carrot."

The less common "birds-nest" name is a description of what the flower head looks like once it has been properly pollinated by the more than fifty insect species such as wasps, ants, flies, and beetles that are attracted to it. Then it closes up to protect its ripening seeds. Over the next three weeks, the "birds-nest" will turn a crispy brown, and as the seeds set, they will exude a volatile oil resembling turpentine that discourages any disturbance by birds or mice. Finally, the seeds mature and the flower head loosens up enough that the seeds are able to sail over the fields in the slightest breeze.

The beauty and intricacy of Queen Anne's lace can best be appreciated with a hand lens. Magnified, it is easy to see that each large flower is composed of many flower heads or umbels, each of which, in turn, is supported by a stem that resembles an umbrella spoke.

The individual florets in each umbel have five petals with a selection of shapes similar to those of sassafras leaves. Some are ovals, some right-handed or left-handed mittens, and still others are heart-shaped. In the center of over half the large composite blossoms of Queen Anne's lace is a single purple, red, or sometimes pink floret. That blossom has been called a "jewel" or the "royal purple," and the English used to believe that if they ate it they would contract pleurisy.

One researcher claims that the average Queen Anne's lace measures three inches across and has seventy-five smaller umbels with a total of two thousand five hundred florets. In the interest of science, I checked out a typical Queen Anne's lace blossom from our meadow and found that it did, indeed, measure almost three inches across, but it contained only thirty-nine smaller umbels. I did not have the patience or eyesight to count each floret. Whatever the total, though, there is no doubt that every plant produces hundreds of seeds.

Those seeds, wild food enthusiast Euell Gibbons claims, are an excellent substitute for caraway in baking. In his book *Stalking the Healthful Herbs,* he also promotes carrot seed tea, which he makes by pouring a pint of boiling water over both a tablespoon of crushed Queen Anne's lace seeds and one of anise seeds. The tea is not only flavorful, according to Gibbons, but it aids in digestion. In addition, he makes a tea of Queen Anne's lace foliage and boils up its young roots as a vegetable.

I have made no culinary experiments with Queen Anne's lace, but when the boys were young, we tried to improve on its beauty. We put the cut blossoms with their stems into individual water glasses and added a few drops of food coloring. Within twenty-four hours we had a rainbow of blue, pink, yellow, and green Queen Anne's laces to mix with the white ones. It always seemed like magic to the boys.

Later today, Bruce and David brought me the Acadian flycatcher nest, now empty, which was woven of bare hemlock twigs and spider webs as far as I could tell. The nest is destined for a nature center in the valley where it will be on display for schoolchildren to see.

Knowing that time is running out to hear wood thrush song, I took an evening walk. Along the Short Circuit Trail I counted three wood thrushes singing at once, answering one another or dueting, each song coming from a different direction. They passed me gently from singer to singer and I felt as if I was being borne up by angel song in a green wood.

JULY 24. I walked quietly along the Short Circuit Trail near ten o'clock this morning and heard an unfamiliar-sounding rustle in the underbrush, so I stopped and waited. Out trotted a porcupine. It never did see me and went trundling down the trail toward the power line right-of-way as I followed undetected about fifteen feet behind it. It walked like a miniature bear, its front feet turned out, its rear end waddling purposefully from side to side, its quills surrounding it like a barbed halo of protection. Occasionally it stopped to sniff a shrub, but it seemed more interested in moving ahead than in eating. After I followed it for the equivalent of a city block, it suddenly swung up into the woods at the edge of the power line right-of-way and silently disappeared.

That was the first time I've ever watched a porcupine move except in a tree. They walk up on their legs, keeping their body and tail well above the ground and, like bears, move faster than their lumbering gait might suggest. The lesson to me is to continue to identify every noise in the underbrush. They aren't always made by eastern towhees, ovenbirds, chipmunks, deer, or gray squirrels. Occasionally they will be turtles, raccoons, fox squirrels, bears, porcupines, or who knows what.

Already the insect nightly chorus, which began hesitantly on July 15 with a couple of katydids, has quickly gained momentum. Tonight the mountain pulsated with the throbbing rhythm of singing insects—crickets, katydids, grasshoppers—

a veritable band of drummers, sometimes with a counterpoint of wailing screech owls, all played by the light of flickering fireflies. How wonderful the nights are, warm and full of
rhythm, music, and light.

JULY 25. Most of the field wildflowers provide food for
other creatures. This morning I watched a male American
goldfinch feed on dame's rocket seed. Bouncing bet attracted
silver-spotted skippers and a black swallowtail butterfly while
Joe Pye weed appealed to great-spangled fritillaries.

Then I encountered a patch of golden-yellow, common St.
John's wort (*Hypericum perforatum*), an immigrant species
that thrives in fields. It seemed to be devoid of feeding insects. Most insects avoid St. John's wort because it emits a
toxic chemical called hypericin, hence its genus name. Hypericin is made and stored in the leaves, flowers, and stem glands
of St. John's wort and slowly poisons a predator.

However, it depends on sunlight to activate it so some insects can resist its toxicity by clever ruses. Butterfly or moth
larvae that roll or fold a leaf and bind it with silk to cover
themselves or sew leaves to form a shelter can eat St. John's
wort from within because they are shielded from sunlight.
Stem borers and leaf miners are also protected from the sun.
The tough outer layer of several adult beetles in the genus
Chrysolina screen out sunlight. The soft-bodied larvae of
Chrysolina hyperici eat inside the leaf buds of St. John's wort
or feed openly on the plant only at dawn. In addition, they
contain a large amount of beta carotene that combats photo-
toxicity. So, no matter how much a plant evolves to resist
predators, there are always a few that can circumvent their
prey's resistance.

Humans have recently been taking St. John's wort to fight
mild depression. They too must stay out of the sun to avoid
triggering hypericin. This seems counterproductive to me. I
would become even more depressed if I were forced to stay

inside. It is the bright sunshine that continually elevates my spirits. After a succession of gloomy, overcast days, my mood matches the weather. Only sunshine cures my depression. Yet so many people spend most of their lives inside under artificial light even in the summer. Perhaps those with mild depression would benefit from frequent walks in the sunlight, especially on such a spectacular summer day as this one.

JULY 26. I sat at the edge of the milkweed patch underneath a small wild apple tree that provided enough shade so I could enjoy the spectacle before me.

Butterflies were the main attraction and many of those that feed on milkweed nectar are orange and black, a striking contrast to the dark rose and dusky pink of milkweed flowers. Monarch butterflies were particularly numerous because they lay their eggs on the undersides of milkweed leaves so the larvae, when they hatch, are able to feed on the only food plant they can eat.

Monarchs were also the largest of the orange and black butterflies and not only chased each other away from the patch but also the several fritillary species that adorned the flowers. Nevertheless, the fritillaries persisted in feeding longer than other butterflies and sorted out by size from the largest—the great-spangled—to the medium-sized—the meadow—to the smallest—the tawny.

Pairs of cabbage butterflies frequently visited the patch along with the swiftly flying, silver-spotted skippers and several dainty, coral hairstreaks. Earlier in the season, when the blossoms first opened, tiger swallowtails were common, but as the blooming season waned and seedpods began to form lower down on the reddish stems beneath the blossoms, there were no more tiger swallowtails.

Bumblebees, several species of flies, and honeybees also like the nectar of milkweed flowers, and hundreds of them kept up a steady hum as I sat there. Twice a bumblebee flew up to my face in what seemed to be a blustering attempt to dislodge me, but I stayed rooted to the spot, my head constantly pivoting, watching the action.

Three beetle species, again adorned in orange and black, fed and mated on milkweed leaves. One pair of bright orange beetles with black spots, the milkweed beetle (*Tetraopes femoratus*), mated on the underside of a leaf. While the female ate the leaf, the male remained firmly in mating position, leading me to the anthropomorphic assumption that the female was more interested in food than sex.

The common milkweed, *Ascelpias syrica,* is just one of seven pink/dark rose species found in the eastern United States. There are also two white species and the most spectacular milkweed of all, the bright orange butterflyweed.

Milkweed is useful in every stage of its existence. Both the young sprouts and pods can be cooked as a vegetable. The silky hairs of the seedpods were once used to stuff pillows and mattresses or mixed with flax or wool and woven into cloth. Our ancestors even manufactured paper from its stalks. They also believed in its medicinal value, using an extract of milkweed for asthma, dyspepsia, and coughs. For this reason its genus name, *Asclepias,* honors a Greek physician.

I have protected this particular patch, just below the barn along the driveway, from the brush cutter on Bruce's tractor so each year it spreads a little further. Scattered plants have emerged as far as the garage and beyond that, where our old garden used to grow, another patch has sprung up. I will probably defend that one as well since, in my opinion, you can't have too much milkweed to observe if you are a naturalist.

JULY 27. Most people would probably agree that there is no morality, as we understand it, in the natural world. The weaker are eaten by the stronger and no one creature is more important in the overall scheme than another.

Human beings, though, often have trouble with this concept, especially when a more cuddly creature, such as a baby cottontail rabbit, is killed by an animal perceived to be less desirable, say a red fox or a great horned owl. Should humans intervene when they can in what they judge, by their standards, to be repugnant to their value system? Or has it been such continual interference by well-meaning people through the ages who think they can fix up or improve on nature that has put the survival of our natural world in the peril it is today? For those of us who ponder such questions it is especially challenging to face a true-life situation and, later, to defend our actions to people who would have chosen a different course.

Living on a Pennsylvania mountaintop surrounded by woods and fields, we sometimes witness what Tennyson called "nature red in tooth and claw." Occasionally we have the option of playing God by intervening on the side of creatures that human beings consider defenseless.

Such a choice faced us this afternoon when David first spotted a five-foot-long, black rat snake coiled behind the ash barrel next to our front door. We assumed it was the resident snake who has lived for several years in a hole in our old farmhouse foundations. Because it is an efficient rat killer, we have always welcomed it. Keeping our distance, we admired its two-inch girth, its handsome, shiny-black back and white belly, and its sinuous body. An hour and a half later, when we next saw it, we laughed aloud. Sprawled full-length along the back porch railing, it was the picture, so we thought, of snaky indolence.

Although David is not afraid of snakes, he did make an instant decision not to sit in his usual chair next to the railing but on the back steps instead. That, it turned out, was a good choice because the snake suddenly slithered over onto the chair and from there twined itself across and down a wicker footstool. It then climbed up the side of the house and along the bottom edge of the kitchen door window, pausing to peer inside at me as I prepared dinner. To see that serpentine head looking in like a nosy neighbor also struck us as humorous, and we began to wonder if there was more to this snake than we had thought.

The snake backed down to the porch floor again and slithered across it to the other railing, which it climbed. I knew then what was motivating it. The creature was hungry, and it had seen parent house wrens feeding their almost-fledged family of five in the hollow post at the end of that railing. I was almost certain that their nest was impregnable, even to a snake, because back in June, when the parents were raising their first family of five nestlings, the only way we had been able to see them was to climb up a stepladder with a flashlight and mirror and peer at the lit reflection of nestlings crammed a couple of feet down into the dark post.

As I suspected, the snake could not climb the smooth square post and so it rippled down across the open outside cellar door, along the sidewalk beneath the porch, and finally out into the grass. It was 6:40 by then and time for us to eat. Besides, it looked as if the snake had given up. However, after dinner Bruce spotted it back up in the corner of the porch ceiling near the house, and all three of us settled down to watch what turned out to be as exciting as an adventure film.

Cautiously the snake climbed onto the latticework below the porch eaves and then looped itself up and over onto the newly shingled porch roof, staying close to the house because it could not get a good grip on the smooth surface of the steeply sloping roof. Then it slowly crawled over to Bruce's second story study window, where it raised its body up to look in several times before looping itself over and around the wooden shutters.

By this time the men were certain the snake could have no interest in the wren nestlings far below, but neither the wrens nor I agreed. As I watched, the snake, still pressed closely to the house, slithered determinedly over to my study window. I realized then that without our intervention the youngsters were doomed. What looked like delaying tactics on the part of the snake was actually a thorough investigation of the possible ways it might move safely down that roof and into the hollow post.

Once again probing with weaving head and flickering tongue, the snake looked through the study screen and behind both shutters before anchoring its long tail around a shutter hook. With that support, it began a slow, catty-corner movement down the porch roof, inching its questing head forward in search of a surface rough enough to cling to. At last it found a few scattered small twigs that had fallen from the poplar tree overhead, and by carefully angling its body along each knobby twig, it moved ever closer to the edge of the porch and the post.

Finally its tail let go of the shutter and with a couple of slides and wriggles it was across the roof and into the rain gutter. From the gutter it was only six inches to the latticework above the hollow post that held the wrens, but first the snake had to get out of that leaf-clogged gutter. As it slowly slithered back and forth, still trapped in the gutter, the house wren parents, who had been watching from the nearby grape tangle along with a seemingly sympathetic but silent gray catbird, flew nervously to the side of the chimney, then to the edge of the bow window, and finally back again to the grape tangle, their attention focused on the determined snake.

Several times that snake, still in the gutter, passed the porch post containing the nestlings, and once again the men doubted its ability to find those birds. The wren parents and I knew better. In less than five minutes the snake paused in the gutter, positioned itself directly opposite the hollow post entrance, and after hooking its tail around a gutter strut, flung the rest of its body onto the latticework. From there it took the snake only a few seconds to thrust its head and half of its body down into the post while its tail stayed securely anchored to the strut.

For at least ten minutes, no one moved. Not the snake, the parent birds, or us. Finally the parents landed on the latticework, coming within a few inches of the lower end of the snake, and scolded but did not touch it. Only after the deed was done and the snake withdrew its head did the parents attack it, diving and hitting its head several times. Beaks open, tails vibrating, chittering loudly, they were bundles of parental fury, but they were too late. Their nestlings had formed only the barest of bulges in the snake's body, and their own harassing seemed to make no impression on the cold-blooded creature at all.

Slowly the snake pulled itself across the latticework and into the gutter and again it coursed back and forth, this time looking for a way down to the ground. First it tried to descend a corrugated pipe attached to a porch post beyond the outside cellar door entrance. That proved to be too smooth for it, so again it retreated to the gutter. Next it returned to the hollow post that had held the nestlings and sent its head down the outside of the post to investigate the possibilities.

At last it discovered the thermometer mounted halfway between the top of the post and the porch railing and, keeping its tail looped around the gutter strut, stretched its body down to the thermometer and twined around it before pulling its tail behind it. From there it was an easy matter for the snake to land on the railing and crawl catty-corner down the open cellar trap door and then to squeeze into a narrow gap between the outside cellar door cement steps and the porch. Despite what had first looked like an impossible task, it had taken the snake one hour and forty minutes, from the time David had first rediscovered it on the back porch, to figure out both a way to get to the birds and then a way to get back to the ground.

The parent wrens returned one last time to check the nest,

but there was only silence. Their second little family was gone, and I, for one, had found it difficult to root for the snake or to dismiss it as nature's way. No matter how much my mind argued that no one creature, going about its business as nature has designed it to do, should be blamed for its behavior, and that all creatures, predator and prey, have a place in the earth's wondrous scheme, I could not feel much empathy for that snake with its unblinking eyes, moving implacably toward those helpless nestlings. Yet at no time did any of us consider killing the black snake to save the birds, even though we liked their cheerful natures and continually warbling songs. Despite passively watching the drama before us, we kept hoping the snake would give up. On the other hand, we realized how lucky we had been to witness a predator actually stalking and eating its prey.

We do not believe in making judgments about the forces of nature. Although we may not be as personally fond of reptiles as we are of birds, to have interfered on the side of the birds struck us as an arrogant act—a presumption on our part that we are wiser than nature. To tinker with what appears to human eyes as a heartless, amoral system seems to be an inherent characteristic of humanity. It is, many people insist, what separates us from the beasts.

Even though we manage birds to some extent on our own land by cutting our meadows every five years to attract meadow as well as woods species, by feeding birds in the winter, and by trying to grow shrubs and trees attractive to birds, we do not believe in favoring one wild creature over the other. In the case of the nestlings and the snake, respect for the intricate web of life forced us to applaud the winner even though we had been rooting for the losers.

JULY 28. It was cool and clear at seven with the sun just topping Laurel Ridge and flooding the front porch with light. I positioned the chaise longue to face the lilac bushes at the left side of the porch, but I still had a wide view of the lawn, the driveway, the guest house, and the black locust trees.

The morning chorus of birds is not as varied as in June. Nevertheless, I heard eastern wood pewees and eastern phoebes, song sparrows and eastern towhees, common yellowthroats and gray catbirds, northern cardinals and tufted titmice—songs enough for a morning awakening.

The barn swallows, parents and offspring, lined up on the telephone wire leading past the barn and kept up a steady chittering. They also made frequent forays over the field to snatch up flying insects. This year there were four nestings—two in the lower part of the barn and two in the upper—and I counted twenty-one barn swallows at a time on the wires.

Next came the white-breasted nuthatches and black-capped chickadees in from the woods, noisy with arrival calls, free from care now that their youngsters are on their own. Amazing how they disappear from sight and sound for two months and then reappear to fill the song vacuum left by those migrants who have already ceased singing for the season.

A young phoebe practiced insect catching—first from a small locust branch on the ground, then from the lowest limb of the crab apple tree, and finally from the Japanese barberry hedge near the springhouse. Another young phoebe landed on a black walnut branch beside the porch, looked me over, and then took a flying swipe through a corner of the porch before landing awkwardly in the pachysandra patch.

A house wren flew in silently, alighted on a porch chair, twitched its tail, flew to the railing, extracted an insect, then was off again.

I got up to shift my seat and to my right just over the edge of the porch, a woodchuck ran from the edge of the herb bed, where it had been eating, into the bank of crown vetch. I watched the movement of the vetch until the creature emerged from the other side, froze for a few seconds, then made its final dive into the grape tangle where it has a den.

Because I was looking closely I spotted the bark-colored brown creeper land quietly on a locust branch and spiral up it. Then a young song sparrow attracted my attention as it poked along the ground, flew up to a locust branch, and groomed its feathers, its legs backlit by the red glow of the strengthening sun.

One house wren was joined by another and they flitted from black walnut to locust tree. Both were young, both were inexperienced, and finally they separated, the one toward the grape tangle, the other toward the driveway, neither seeming to respond to the continual wren song from the edge of the wood. Both were probably offspring from the first brood of the back porch house wrens.

As a finale a young catbird landed on the porch at my feet, flicked its tail, and was off to the lilac bush.

By 8:30 the show was over, but the quiet watching left me with a sense of peace and the strength to face my mundane tasks with equanimity.

JULY 29. I sweated as I walked this warm, humid morning. Along Laurel Ridge Trail a pair of hooded warblers chipped and performed their distraction display, flying within five feet of me. This is where I always run into frantic hooded warbler parents, year after year, so somewhere in the underbrush hooded warbler fledglings hide.

Then, a little further along the trail, the woods suddenly rustled with at least a dozen masked shrews running over the forest floor. I stood and watched until they noticed and disappeared into the leaf duff. Usually I see such behavior in April and always assumed it was courtship chasing; since masked shrews breed from spring until autumn, this could be the second courtship.

Along Sapsucker Ridge Trail, a swarm of flies alerted me to

an enormous white stinkhorn mushroom with a beige head, its sticky head covered with flies and a couple of aggressive carrion beetles—*Silpha americana.*

Finally, as I walked past our old garden site, two startled songbirds flew up out of the weeds at my side and landed on an open tree branch at the edge of the woods, chattering loudly. As I looked down at the grass from where they had flown up and then considered getting out my binoculars to figure out if they were chipping sparrows, a sharp-shinned hawk streaked across First Field and snatched one of the birds without a pause in its flight, gone as quickly as it had appeared. Its swift, silent, deadly accuracy has resulted in the appropriate nickname "bullet hawk" and provided quick but exciting drama. I have often seen sharpies dive after feeder birds in the winter and miss. That was the first hit I have witnessed.

JULY 30. By the end of July, some mourning doves may be raising their third family of the year. Although they usually lay two or, at the most, three eggs, they make up for their small families by raising more broods than other birds, and they begin, in central Pennsylvania, as early as April 4.

Mourning doves start their bumbling courtship rites a few days after they return from winters spent in the southeastern United States or central America. While the female can make faint cooing noises, it is the male we hear giving the characteristic mournful call from Sapsucker Ridge in mid-March.

Our mountain does not have ideal nesting habitat for mourning doves but we usually have at least one couple nesting at the edge of Sapsucker Ridge woods each summer. They don't mind fragmented habitat, even suburban backyards, along with orchards, shelterbelts, edges of woods, pastures, and fields. Their favorite nesting trees are spruce and white pines, but they will also settle for hardwood trees and even shrubs.

Calling what they construct a nest is probably an insult to

self-respecting, careful nest builders such as Baltimore orioles or American robins. Mourning doves seem to pride themselves in doing as little work as possible. The male gathers nesting materials, one straw or pine needle at a time, and gallantly presents each piece to his mate who is waiting at the nesting site to construct the haphazard nest. They choose the flat bough of a tree and lay out the nesting materials in platform style, although some nests have been found along roadsides, on the ground, or in rainspouts. They also use old American robin, common grackle, and gray catbird nests. Unfortunately, their choice of nesting sites, and the flimsy structures they construct, often lead to disaster either at the hands of a strong wind or a determined predator.

However, gender equality was long ago acknowledged in the mourning dove world. They have neatly divided up all duties in brooding, feeding, and caring for the young. The male incubates the eggs from approximately 8:30 A.M. until 4:30 P.M. each day. Then the female takes over for the night. Neither bird feeds the other at the nest. Each does its own feeding and watering in two short breaks while brooding.

Equal rights are even more obvious once the young doves hatch. Both parents produce "pigeon milk" which is secreted from the lining of their crops in the upper part of their digestive tracts. They pump this milk, which is similar to rabbit milk, from their crops and into the bases of their bills where the young reach it by inserting the tips of their bills just above a red marking on the adult birds' faces. The famous bird photographer, Frederick Kent Truslow, once photographed young doves nursing and reported that he could hear sucking noises eight feet away in his blind.

By the time their young are five days old, the parents are weaning their young to seeds, and when they leave the nest, at thirteen to seventeen days of age, their diet is similar to that of their parents. Ninety-seven percent of their food consists of weed seeds found on or near the ground—chiefly grass seeds, hemp, and green foxtail. One stomach of a mourning dove contained 6,400 foxtail seeds. They also glean wheat and corn seeds, particularly if they choose to winter here, as eleven did last winter, flying up from the valley to feast on cracked corn beneath our feeders every day.

Many people think of mourning doves as boring birds because they are so common, but I admire them for their "equal rights" and their faithfulness to each other through the entire breeding season. Seen in the right light, they are beautiful birds as well, with their rosy pink breasts and shades of violet and blue in their gray coats.

Best of all, though, are their songs. As Dr. Wallace Craig put it in his article, "The Expressions of Emotion in the Mourning Dove," "Some pigeons have more elaborate songs, but for romantic sweetness there is no pigeon song I ever heard which can approach that of our mourning dove" (401).

JULY 31. Foggy, with occasional stray breezes that shake rain off the trees from a nighttime shower. It was difficult to stop on my walk for even a few seconds without hearing the whine of a mosquito in my ear. Not yet Maine-proportion mosquitoes, or even New Jersey; but the wet summer has been favorable for mosquito breeding. As usual, though, the cherry woods were bugfree, so I could sit and listen to the pattering of fog droplets in the misty green forest.

At the top of a Norway spruce I saw a cedar waxwing with nest materials in its beak, a part of a larger flock. Indigo buntings and eastern towhees also sang there.

The mosquitoes attacked again as I descended First Field in the mist. Why do I force myself out every day despite the weather? What rewards will I reap?

As if in answer to my unspoken questions, a black animal leaped toward me. At first I thought it was a rat. Then I saw its long, furry tail, lean body, stubby legs, and weasel-like face. I froze and it reached my feet before it saw me, paused, and then silently turned right into the field grasses. A few minutes later, there was another movement to the side and slightly in back of me to the left. Before that animal came into view, it must have scented me because it suddenly turned and ran in the opposite direction.

After some consideration, I decided the animal could only have been a long-tailed weasel even though they are a deep chocolate brown with white or yellow bellies. The wet field had slicked down and darkened its coat so that it had looked black to me in the dim light. It was my first sight ever of this mostly nocturnal animal who had chosen to hunt on this dark day, thus providing an exciting climax to an eventful July.

August

There was a child went forth every day,
And the first object he look'd upon, that object he became,
And that object became part of him for the day or a certain
  part of the day,
Or stretching cycles of years.

Walt Whitman

AUGUST 1. At first I thought the monotonous, high-pitched "peer" call belonged to an aberrant eastern wood pewee who could only sing part of its repetitious song. One morning the call came from the dead oak at the edge of the woods. From the house I quickly spotted again the speckled-breasted juvenile broad-winged hawk perched near the top of the tree making the plaintive shriek. Another broad-winged hawk answered it.

I went outside to get a closer look. Just like the juvenile I had watched along Ten Springs Trail the other week (and probably the same youngster), it was not frightened by me. After the merest glance in my direction, it continued to call, even when a gray catbird landed beside it and started to scold. This is typical broad-winged hawk behavior. Ornithologist Arthur Cleveland Bent once called it the gentlest and friendliest of hawks, and I am inclined to agree.

Why have they been screaming all day, every day, for weeks

now? Bent claims they cry only when they are alarmed near their nest. Sometimes my head reverberates with the sound of the repetitive shrieking. The famous naturalist John Burroughs considered it "the smoothest, most ear-piercing note I know of in the woods" (in Bent, pt. 2, 248), an opinion I concur with. My own guess about the constant calling I am hearing is that, like screech-owl families when their young are newly fledged, they continue calling so they can keep in touch with each other in the dense woods.

These are, after all, deep woods birds who prefer to nest in coniferous and mixed stands in heavily forested areas of more than one hundred acres. They especially like a wild, rocky, wooded ravine above a small stream in a mixed hardwood forest. One writer calls it a "bird of the wilderness," and another claims it prefers a quiet woods remote from human dwellings, not, obviously, the case with these broad-winged hawks.

I have not found this year's nest, but a decade and a half ago, when we had our heaviest gypsy moth infestation, because the trees were so stripped of their foliage I easily located a broad-winged hawk nest at the top of a large oak tree only a few hundred feet from the stream. Sometimes they reuse nests, but when I checked that nest over the next several years, I never found another family.

Broad-winged hawks don't attack domestic poultry but instead eat squirrels, chipmunks, mice, rats, meadow voles, cottontail rabbits, snakes, toads, grasshoppers, and moth larvae, among other foods. Breeding bird surveys of Pennsylvania over the last thirty years have found that the ridge-and-valley province where we live has the highest number of nesting broad-winged hawks in the state.

Although they like heavy forest cover while nesting, the broad-winged hawks here seem to prefer open areas, such as the clear-cut and our fields, once the birds have fledged. This year a youngster circles above our barn and house by 8:30

every morning. Often it is joined by its parents in a swirling ballet punctuated by shrieks. Barn swallows or other song-birds harry the juvenile, but it merely shakes its head and ignores them. It needs all the flying practice it can get before it embarks on its long migration to Brazil in September.

AUGUST 2. The eastern screech owls began their quavering, down-scale trilling this year at dusk on July 28. According to screech owl researcher Frederick R. Gehlbach, such calling is a sign that dispersing screech owl youngsters are about, triggering the mature male screech owls to defend their territories from the young interlopers.

Although the down-scale trilling is the most common noise screech owls make, they do screech when frightened. They also hoot, bark, chatter, and clack their bills together when threatened by predators.

Both Bruce and I can testify to all those noises plus others that are beyond description because this evening screech owls congregated in the woods below our house and set up such a caterwauling that the deer began snorting in fright and finally ran off.

Even when we turned on the spotlights we could not see anything. We were almost certain, however, that they were screech owls, since interspersed with all the weird noises were the almost unending familiar screech owl trills. The cacophony continued off and on for over an hour and a half, prompting Bruce to wonder whether our neighbors would ever quiet down so we could get some sleep.

Apparently male screech owls have lower-pitched trills than females and do most of the trilling, since they use it in territorial defense and in communication with their mates. The larger, heavier females are the chief defenders of the nest and nestlings so they are more likely to hoot and bark. Probably what we heard were all sexes and ages mixing it up.

In addition to the usual down-scale trilling of late summer, screech owls also emit a sweet, melodious, one-pitch trill in late winter when they are declaring ownership over their cavity nest. Since they mate for life, they don't have to call to attract a mate.

They also don't build their own nests. Instead, they take over abandoned cavity nests of northern flickers or pileated woodpeckers and lay four to six white eggs, often at two- or three-day intervals. Usually the female begins brooding as soon as she lays her first egg. From then until a week after the owls hatch—approximately five weeks—her mate provides all her food. She only leaves the nest once a day, at dusk, to drink and defecate.

The mate she depends on is at least 17 percent smaller than she is with 25 percent less body weight per unit of wing surface area. In fact, female screech owls choose the smallest males they can find as mates.

Researcher Gehlbach, after studying screech owls for nineteen years, believes that the smaller the male, the less food he needs for himself because he expends less energy in flying. Therefore he burns up fewer calories. As a consequence, he will provide more food for his mate.

The heavier the female, on the other hand, the better she is at defending the nestlings, laying the maximum number of fertile eggs, and raising her youngsters to maturity. So, for screech owls, small males and large females or "reversed size dimorphism," as scientists call it, makes sense.

Screech owls like open habitat for nesting, especially wooded riparian areas. The youngsters we have seen over the years have been either in hemlock trees in the hollow beside the stream or at the magic place close to First Field.

Although rodents of all species and insects such as grasshoppers are preferred food, screech owls also eat songbirds, a habit that does not endear them to some bird lovers. One researcher, Althea Sherman of Iowa, spent many days and nights observing a screech owl family who nested in a box she provided. She claimed that screech owls particularly relished dark-eyed juncos and song sparrows. Other screech owl observers were relieved to find a preference for the alien and ubiquitous house sparrows. Then there was the screech owl, back in 1931, who went down a New Jersey chimney and ate the family canary.

AUGUST 3. I was awakened before dawn, when the lawn was still splashed by moonlight, by a mosquito buzzing in my ear. Making the best of it, I listened to the greatly diminished dawn bird chorus. First an eastern towhee, second a Carolina wren, third a northern cardinal. Then a brief cascade by an indigo bunting, followed by a common yellowthroat and a song sparrow. Finally the dawn was silent again as if brief bursts of song in tribute to the light were all the birds needed to do now that the frenzied business of courtship, nesting, and raising families had wound down.

Later I discovered a poem written by William Cullen Bryant called "To A Musquito." The title alone amused me. I never knew Bryant had a sense of humor, but I was convinced by the following lines:

> Fair insect! That, with thread-like legs spread out,
> And blood-extracting bill, and filmy wing,
> Does murmur, as thou slowly sail'st about.
> . . . .
> Thou'rt welcome to the town—but why come here? (187, 189)

Exactly my sentiments. Especially at dawn when I'm still sleeping.

It was even worse during my walk. The July 19 flood has brought about an unprecedented hatching of floodwater mosquitoes, most likely *Aedes trivittatus,* which likes wooded wet areas, and *Aedes vexans,* which likes grassy areas. Mosquitoes rose from the earth like a malevolent mist. They circled about me, a chorus of singing harpies searching for vulnerable places to stab me and suck my blood. No relief from them, not even in the black cherry woods, not even covered with foul-smelling insect repellent. Being in the woods is no longer a pleasure, but a penance. Nothing stirred except a singing red-eyed vireo, a black-and-white warbler, and a tapping downy woodpecker.

Then, when I reached First Field, a foggy, warm breeze blew away the mosquitoes. Birds sang, flowers bloomed, and no mosquitoes whined. Finally I could stop walking fast and swinging my arms, and slow down to appreciate what I was seeing and hearing. Field sparrows, common yellowthroats, eastern towhees, black-capped chickadees, and tufted titmice sang and called. Butter-and-eggs and Queen Anne's lace were the dominant field flowers in bloom, even as the last daisies faded and the first early goldenrod appeared.

AUGUST 4. Today, when Bruce set out to cut the lower half of First Field, I explored a small marsh near the frog pond that supports a heavy growth of sedges, a clump of cattails, a few rushes, and those denizens of watery places—dragonflies.

The dragonfly species I saw was the white-tailed skimmer (*Plathemis lydia*) who has black splotches on gossamer wings. Skimmers, like all dragonfly species, are members of the large order *Odonata* and spend much of their lives as nymphs in the water.

After approximately twelve molts, they finally emerge from a pond or stream, rest on its banks, squeeze out of their last skin, and expand into tenerals—dragonflies whose bodies are still soft and flying abilities weak. During this stage, which lasts several days, birds prey heavily on them. When at last they develop into hard-bodied, strong-flying dragonflies, they are ready to mate.

Female dragonflies have only a month to mate and lay their eggs. They can also store male sperm. This ability leads to a mating practice common among many insects and some mammals called "sperm competition." The last male to mate with a female will father most of her offspring.

Dragonfly males engage in one of two kinds of "mate-guarding" to make certain females whom they mate with will not mate with others before laying eggs. The first, called "contact guarding," is when a male clasps the female he has just mated with behind her head as she moves along and lays her eggs. In the second, "noncontact guarding," the male hovers over the female and drives off other potential rivals while she lays her eggs.

White-tailed skimmers are "noncontact" guarders, according to researcher Vicky McMillan who spent June through August beside an upper New York state pond studying several marked male white-tailed skimmers. She discovered that male skimmers remained sexually active over several weeks as they visited their chosen mating area at the pond for hours every day.

Females, on the other hand, visited the pond infrequently and for only a few minutes, long enough to mate and lay their eggs. They spent the rest of their time eating and resting in nearby fields. As soon as a female arrived at the pond, a male would grab her firmly behind the head with his claspers at the tip end of his abdomen. Then, because the male's penis is in the front of his abdomen, the female would bend the end of her abdomen, where her genital opening is, upward to reach the male's penis, putting them in a "wheel-position," and they would mate in three seconds.

After he released her in a good egg-laying area, she would dip her abdomen repeatedly into the pond water, releasing streams of eggs that sank to the bottom while her mate hovered above her and chased out other males. Occasionally she would be interrupted just before or during egg-laying by several males, which her "guard" would be unable to keep away.

When this happened she would either fly to the pond bank

and perch motionless—which apparently makes her undesirable to both her "guard" and other males—and then return to lay her eggs, still "guarded," after the other males had retreated. Or she would flee the pond altogether without laying many or any eggs, depending on how severely she was harassed.

Eighty percent of the time, however, a female white-tailed skimmer completed her egg laying without harassment, a process that would take four or five minutes once she selected her site and began hovering over it. Her mate would guard her closely until the end of her egg laying if there was great competition from other males. If there was little or no competition, males often tried to impregnate a second female while still guarding a first.

In other words, male dragonflies adjust their behavior to suit the circumstances. How amazing that even the so-called lowly insects are not mere automatons in their life functions.

AUGUST 5. Who would have thought the common forest snail could have appeal? Yet when I first saw it this afternoon, moving rapidly along a leaf, I was surprised. There seemed to be both purpose and energy in its actions and my presence did not make it retreat into its shell. Instead, it waved its long antennae as I peered at it through my hand lens.

On a whim, I plucked the leaf and carried it and the snail back home with me to show the family. I put it down on the kitchen table and it quickly moved to the edge of the leaf and onto the table. Somewhat hesitantly, I put my right forefinger in front of it, which it immediately climbed up. I could feel the suction from its pinpoint-sized mouth as it searched for food. I also watched it excreting mucus from a gland just behind its mouth so it could glide smoothly over my finger.

After a few circlings of that finger, the snail moved purposefully to the tip where it extended its upper pair of antennae toward my second finger. Stretching the front part of its body across a one-inch gap, its head reached that next finger, but I expected the snail to be unbalanced when its shell crossed the gap. Instead the shell dropped down a half-inch and for a few breathless seconds, the snail's head was on my second finger, its tail was on my forefinger, and its shell dangled in between. With what seemed no effort at all, the snail pulled the rest of itself onto my third finger and, finally, across and down to my little finger.

All of us were amazed at its boldness, agility, and speed, and I found myself charmed by the creature. From tip to tip, its body measured two inches and its larger antennae, which had primitive eyes at the ends of them, were a half-inch long. Below those large antennae, near the mouth, were two very small antennae that are sensitive touch organs.

The mucus the snail had secreted over my fingers dried within a few seconds into a gritty substance that was easily brushed off. Later I learned that it has a high acid content that allows it to dissolve the limestone the snail must ingest during the summer to keep its shell strong.

David suggested that I keep the snail until Bruce came home from the university and could photograph it, so I put it back on the leaf. It immediately withdrew into its shell. When Bruce arrived two hours later, I picked up the round, one-inch, brown-colored shell to show him. I was certain that the snail had retreated for the day and I tried to explain to Bruce how it had performed earlier.

As if on cue, the snail suddenly emerged from its shell and began circling around my forefinger. After two complete cycles, it started up my finger again. Bruce ran for the camera and while he snapped away, the snail repeated the whole routine. When Bruce had taken enough pictures, I put the snail outside on a wild grape leaf and bid it a fond farewell. It never looked back, but glided off at its optimum speed (which I had timed earlier) of one inch every ten seconds.

The whole incident intrigued me, especially when I learned

that snails ordinarily are not active during hot, dry days. Instead they estivate by drawing into their shells and sealing themselves off with a layer of mucus, emerging only during the cooler, more humid evenings to eat and be eaten. They prefer maple and oak hardwood forests where they dine on woodland vegetation and the mycelia of forest fungi. Birds, frogs, toads, snakes, chipmunks, field mice, shrews, and moles dine on snails, which is why most snail shells are empty or broken when they are found in the woods.

Calling my snail an "it" was entirely correct since all snails contain both male and female sex organs. This does not mean that sex is absent from their lives. Twice a year, in spring and fall, snails get an urge to search for other snails. However, they ignore those familiar snails in their own vicinity and go off to look for the mucus trails of strangers.

When one snail discovers a stranger's mucus trail, it follows it until it finds its maker. Then the two snails fondle each other for several hours before shooting one another with a calcareous dart. This triggers the emergence of a sex organ from the right side of each snail's head, which penetrates the other's neck and releases sperm, thereby fertilizing its partner's eggs. After that, they separate, and twelve to fifteen days later, each snail digs its own nest, deposits its speck-sized eggs in it, covers the nest with leaves, and deserts it. In three to four weeks, fully formed tiny snails hatch and crawl out of the nest to begin their own independent lives.

Had it been a damp spring or fall day, I would have related my snail's energetic exploratory actions to its search for a partner. Today, however, it has been hot and dry and it seems as if the snail broke all known snail rules. This only demonstrated how little we understand about the lives of such seemingly simple creatures.

AUGUST 6. Eva rolled from her tummy to her back on our bed today and looked both surprised and pleased with herself. Standing while I hold her is a favorite pastime as she balances on her toes and stretches out her arms like a ballet dancer. She is also beginning to play with her toys and shows great interest in and awareness of everything and everybody around her. Most of all, though, she is a huggable little morsel and she knows it.

Unfortunately, she is susceptible to insect bites and heat and so, because of the plague of mosquitoes, she must stay indoors all day. The rest of the family is also staying close to home because of the mosquitoes. No more meals on the veranda; no more leisurely evenings of conversation and reading outside. Such conditions are reminiscent of our years in Maine when David was a little boy.

Twenty-five years ago, when we prepared to move here after five years in Maine, I described Pennsylvania to four-year-old David as a "bugfree paradise." Already in early June he was covered with black fly bites despite being slathered in Old Woodsman's Fly Dope and swathed in a head net. He knew that our Maine woods continued to be uninhabitable from the Fourth of July until several hard frosts in late September because of the legions of mosquitoes that hatched once the black flies subsided. So when I described the lack of true northwoods black flies and aggressive mosquitoes in Pennsylvania, he told me later that he thought Pennsylvania must be the most wonderful place on earth.

Over the years in Pennsylvania, on humid summer days, larger black flies circled our heads in the woods but rarely bit, and "no-see-ums" did deliver minimal bites. We even saw and killed an occasional mosquito, but they were not in the same league as Maine black flies and mosquitoes. We were certain that we had found as close to a bugfree paradise as possible on this earth. With the advent of the floodwater mosquitoes, David's insect phobia has returned. And Luz, because she comes from a country where the threat of disease from mosquitoes is constant, protects Eva from every mosquito that buzzes in her direction during their short walks each day from the guest house to the main house for meals.

AUGUST 7. On the first day of August Bruce reported what he thought were screaming young American kestrels along Laurel Ridge. The next day I went to investigate. Instead of kestrels I found shrieking, recently fledged sharp-shinned hawks—another new breeding species for the mountain. I followed them through the woods as they called and even sat awhile hoping for a good look, but all I saw were brief glimpses.

Today I was luckier. In the same place I had previously heard them, they shrieked again, so I sat down to watch. Almost immediately one landed on a fairly open branch, and I had a good opportunity to study it as it fanned out and preened its tail feathers. It had a faintly striped, square-edged tail rimmed with white, a chestnut back and head with a few white feathers, a white belly, and russet on its flanks—definitely an immature sharpie.

When I moved down into the woods, the sharpies continued calling. I assumed they were objecting to me, but then I discovered an immature sharpie sitting on a dead snag, unaware that I was there.

I lay down on the ground and watched it through my binoculars as it sat quietly for more than half an hour looking around, its feathers and tail blowing in the wind. Finally it started to preen its mottled red-on-white breast feathers for several minutes and then abruptly flew off the snag, yelling. It never did see me.

I was amazed at how long the bird had sat quiet and still, and I was reminded of an article in *National Wildlife* entitled "Life in the Slow Lane" by Grant Sims. He wrote, "Animals, it appears, are capable of just about any adaptation imaginable in order to live the quiet life. Counterintuitive as that notion may seem, biologists have been impressed in the last decade by the discovery that most wildlife spends about two-

thirds of the time quiescent" (18). University of Vermont zo-
ologist Joan Herbers first discovered how much down time
animals spend back in 1980 when she was gathering information on animal foraging activity for a study in the new field of
time-budget analysis. Pulling data together from many scientific field studies she had a "eureka" experience. "It was suddenly obvious that all kinds of creatures were spending most
of their time apparently doing nothing at all," she said (20).
Even high-energy shrews spent only about one-fifth of their
time foraging and 68 percent at rest. Some of what looks like
rest, other researchers have pointed out, actually has evolutionary significance—lions that look like they are lazing
around a water source are actually waiting for prey, for instance—but Herbers insists that, "Some of these animals are
relaxing. They're there because they would prefer to lie
around in the shade on a hot day than to work for a living"
(22). Or they are conserving their strength so they don't burn
up too many calories when food is scarce. In the case of the
sharpies, they probably call loudly when their parents are
near, hoping for food, but when their parents are off hunting,
they take the time to rest.

I was pleased to have positively confirmed the sharp-
shinned hawk as a breeder under the "recently fledged" criterion set out in the *Atlas of Breeding Birds in Pennsylvania*. Lau-
rie Goodrich says in the *Atlas* that the sharpie is a secretive
breeder who likes isolated, large tracts of forest far from human habitation. The area of Laurel Ridge where I found
them is extensively wooded and has the dense canopy sharp-
shinned hawks need, but our house is less than a quarter of a
mile away. Perhaps the sharpies, like other wildlife, are hard-
pressed to find ideal habitat to breed in and so are settling for
whatever they can get.

AUGUST 8. I walked down the hollow road this morning
and wondered why some birds—eastern wood pewees, red-
eyed vireos, northern cardinals, song sparrows, and Carolina

wrens—keep singing long after other birds are silenced for the year.

I climbed up the last sunlit side hollow to sit for awhile and watched insects rise in the sunbeams sifting through the green leaves. The ground near me began to twitter and shake and I knew I was close to the territory of a hyperactive shrew. A few seconds later, twittering loudly, a gray-bodied northern short-tailed shrew emerged from the rock pile behind me and scrambled quickly out of sight farther up the hillside.

It took a little longer for the slow, lethargic mosquitoes to find me, but when they did, I was ready to move back down to the road and follow it to the bottom of the mountain. Then I started walking up the almost-dry stream bed to perform my self-appointed research task for the day—looking for rare plants and salamanders.

Almost immediately I spotted a tiny, light-colored frog who leapt away so fast that I could not identify it. Then I started turning over flattish rocks in moist (but not running water) habitat and discovered a bonanza of northern dusky salamanders, one or two under almost every rock I lifted. When I reached twenty-five and had covered about a twentieth of a mile, I was already tired and had proved my point. Salamanders are plentiful in the hollow still, including the northern two-lined salamanders I also found.

Then I made a second discovery. In that lower part of the hollow, huge jack-in-the-pulpits grow. The berry clusters were still green on the single hip-high plant with leaves one and a half feet long in two sets of three, with fleshy, purple and green stems as thick as my thumb. I also found several smaller plants, with berries, hidden beneath the lush bank of wood ferns. Rotten, fallen nurse logs lay across the stream in several places, all of which supported ferns, foamflowers, and black birch seedlings.

Just as I was getting hungry, I reached the blowdown area at the big pull off and discovered large, black, luscious blackberries hanging down from the stream bank. I ate as many as I could reach without risk to life or limb.

Above the big pull off, where huge tulip and beech trees had fallen, it was very wet, evidently the source of a spring, which is probably what weakened the trees and sent them over. An ovenbird looked as if it were sneaking up and down an exposed tree root, watching me and ducking its head. It was probably a scared youngster now on its own, since adults always leave shortly after they raise their family to maturity. Eastern chipmunks "chunked" at me in a mighty chorus from the mountainside above.

Finally, I pulled myself up the stream bank to the road when I had finished exploring the deepest part of the hollow, what our neighbor Margaret used to call "the dark place." I had had enough of up and over, around and atop so many fallen trees and branches, of upsetting the local bird population no end, and of constant scolding by scarlet tanagers.

As I walked back up the road, within the span of a few hundred feet halfway between the forks and the guest house, no less than three female ruffed grouse cried and displayed and then scuttled across the road and up into the woods, whining all the way. I saw only two almost fully grown youngsters explode from the stream bed, crashing through spicebush as they too fled up into the woods. Were they all that survived from three broods or had I missed some?

AUGUST 9. As we were driving up the hollow road last evening, we saw a small creature bouncing like a ping-pong ball in front of our car.

"Jumping mouse," Bruce commented, before telling me of the nights several years ago when he had counted dozens of them while driving home.

"That was some population explosion," he said.

Today, after he returned from cutting the Far Field, he reported another jumping mouse population explosion—this time at the Far Field. That was when we realized that we have two species of jumping mice on the mountain.

Our hollow mice are woodland jumping mice, *Napaeozapus insignis*. They have slightly longer tails and bodies than their cousins, the meadow jumping mice, *Zapus hudsonius,* that live at the Far Field. Woodland jumping mice also have white-tipped tails and more vibrantly colored bodies—bright orange mixed with brown and black, rather than the yellowish-brown with black-tipped hairs of the meadow jumping mice. Both species share in common white underparts, long hind legs, and a thin tail one and a half times the length of their bodies.

All jumping mice are primarily seed eaters. Second on their preference list are insects. Meadow jumping mice live in wet grasslands and old fields, while woodland jumping mice like deep woodlands close to mountain streams or bogs. Neither species uses runways like most mice species; instead, they hide and feed under heavy vegetation.

While other mice store food for the winter, jumping mice store fat on their bodies so they can hibernate. They lie curled in balls in warm nests below the frost line where they sleep the true sleep of hibernation. Their body temperatures have dropped from ninety-eight degrees Fahrenheit to thirty-three, along with Pennsylvania's other true hibernators—woodchucks and several wintering bat species.

It might seem like a good idea to sleep away the cold months, from late October until late April, living on a fat layer built up in early autumn by eating underground fungi, seeds, and fruits, as woodland jumping mice do. Scientists have found, however, that as many as 75 percent of hibernating woodland jumping mice will not survive until spring, succumbing to starvation, severe cold, or spring flooding of their hillside underground nests.

Soon after they awaken, breeding takes place. The young of the meadow jumping mice, from three to six, are born eighteen days later in well-constructed nests of grass and leaves that are usually placed under a log or in an underground chamber. They produce second and sometimes even third litters later in the summer.

The woodland jumping mice breed a little later and have their three to six young in late June or early July. Sometimes they have a second litter in August as well. It takes twenty-six days for the youngsters' eyes to open and they are not weaned until they are a month old.

Most observers credit woodland jumping mice with having the longest leaps—eight to ten feet—while those of meadow jumping mice seldom exceed three feet. Woodland jumping mice also have a more limited range in the eastern United States—from Maine to North Carolina and west to Wisconsin. The meadow jumping mice live as far north as Hudson Bay, south through South Carolina and Alabama, and west to Iowa and Missouri.

Woodland jumping mice are also known as "kangaroo mice" because of their large hind feet that propel them like children on pogo sticks. Their genus name—*Napaeozapus*—means "a woodland nymph or fairy with very large feet." Seen as bounding black silhouettes in our car headlights, we could almost believe they are related to the wee ones of folklore.

AUGUST 10. I believe we will live on blackberries this winter—not the large, juicy, tart kind, but the smaller, drier, sweeter variety that populate the power line right-of-way and other waste places.

Even as I fought the heat and humidity, brambles that reached out and tore my skin, and all manner of biting, buzzing, and stinging insects while picking this morning, I rejoiced. I was filling the freezer for winter at no expense and without weeding, as I would in a garden. All it required was an outlay of my time and the sacrifice of my skin.

There were other rewards too. It gave me an excuse to stay

outside longer than usual. Picking blackberries is valuable, seasonal work that must be done now when the sun is warm. So every day I choose my blackberry picking time carefully. If it is humid and buggy I am happy to flee back into the house after an exhausting battle with deerflies, mosquitoes, and no-see-ums. If the day is clear, cool, and sunny, I stake my claim and time on every berry patch within a mile radius of our home and I pick and pick and pick.

It is more comfortable to pick when it is cooler because of the protective armor I must wear: a long-sleeved shirt, jeans, and hiking boots. The latter are especially important as I trample new trails through briars and brush in the fields or sweep aside the hay-scented ferns that serve as an understory in the blackberry patches of the power line right-of-way or push my way through the clear-cut area.

As I poked along this morning I surprised other creatures that also like blackberries. Gray catbirds, for instance, nest in the brambles and one kept up a steady scolding as I picked out its patch, but I ignored it. That catbird will be heading south for easy living in a couple of months and has no idea about storing up for winter.

The eastern box turtle that nudged my toe was another matter. It was waiting for berries to drop its way and, of course, it will go nowhere in winter except below the frost line to hibernate. I felt more akin to its need than the catbird's and, besides, no matter how I stretched and strained, I could not reach all the berries that the catbird's wings make accessible to it.

I was even willing to share the harvest with the insects although I divided up in my mind the good and bad insects and preferred the former. I gently brushed away a yellow crab spider, many small, scurrying ants, and several harvestmen, but I rudely shook the imported Japanese beetles from their perches on the leaves and berries.

Despite the noise I made, I startled a deer in the berry

patch near midday. A large buck suddenly surfaced from the fern bed thirty feet away. Since only "mad dogs and Englishmen [and I] work in the midday sun," the buck had probably been resting in the shade. He reared up, snorted, stamped, and fled off into the woods.

So there were other rewards besides the picking and the blackberry pies and cobblers and ice cream and all the other wonderful dishes I can make with blackberries. We will enjoy them fresh now and frozen later. And I have reaped free food, free exercise, and, most of all, free memories for the long winter.

AUGUST II. The cast of wildflowers has changed again. Along the Laurel Ridge Trail this morning I found panicled hawkweed (*Hieracium paniculatum*). This hawkweed, unlike the well-known king devil or yellow hawkweed and the orange hawkweed, is a native species and, as such, has not made itself a pest as the alien species have (in the opinion of farmers). It also prefers open woods to farmers' fields. All the hawkweeds get their English and genus name (*Hieracium* means "hawk") from the belief in England that hawks eat the juice of hawkweeds to sharpen their eyesight.

Another native hawkweed (*Hieracium venosum*) grew along the edge of the Far Field. Known as rattlesnake weed because its purple-veined basal leaves supposedly resemble the skin of a rattlesnake, its leaves are far lovelier than its flowers. For several years its identity puzzled me until at last I caught it in bloom a couple of weeks ago.

Several plants of the alien Deptford pinks (*Dianthus armeria*) added a bright note to the Far Field. Its genus name means "Jove's own flower," which may refer to the vibrancy of its color rather than to its small, undistinguished, five-petalled, half-inch flower.

At the top of First Field yellow wood-sorrel (*Oxalis stricta*) blossomed. This flower, too, is inconspicuous, but its heart-shaped, cloverlike leaflets are distinctive. So are its erect seed-pods on bent stalks that form a sharp angle upward, making the plants easy to identify long after they have bloomed.

Two fawns came bleating into the yard in the late afternoon. They were joined by another fawn and doe and all fed peacefully together in First Field during a downpour. Then the doe kicked up her back legs and ran around the fawns, enticing all of them to do likewise. Was she baby-sitting the twins?

It seemed a miracle that the clouds had disappeared before sunset so that the western horizon was bathed in a pinkish glow. Fireflies flashed on and off and the rising tide of thrumming insects filled the dusk as I walked over the newly mown First Field, waiting for the Perseid meteor shower to begin or, rather, for the sky to darken enough so that I could see it. Mist rose from the hollow and slowly settled over the field or billowed up toward the sky, threatening to obscure our vision.

As the first star appeared overhead, I joined David, who was spread out on a camping pad, at the top of the field. We waited and waited as the few brightest stars blinked in and out of the mist and the heavens flickered with distant lightning. Finally, one meteor flashed across the top of the sky like fireworks and elicited a "Wow!" from both of us. We saw only a few more small ones—about ten—before the misty clouds completely blotted out the night sky. Not once, during any August that we have been here, can I remember really clear skies during the time of the Perseid meteor shower.

AUGUST 12. For the first time in many years, we have shared First Field with a family of American kestrels. Every afternoon for over a month the five of them have gathered on the barn cupola for a "chitter," sounding like a large flock of songbirds. They never stay still for long, though. First one, then another, sails off across the field and perches on power poles or telephone wires, watching for grasshoppers, mice, and crickets, their principal prey during the benign summer months.

Before the American kestrels were more accurately re-named by the American Ornithologists' Union, they were known as sparrow hawks. They are not hawks, however; they are the smallest of our falcons. In winter, when they are hard pressed, they will eat sparrows and other small songbirds, but nicknames such as "mouse hawks" and "grasshopper hawks" more accurately describe their preferred foods. With grass-hoppers at their peak in August and September we always have at least one or two that fly in every day to sit on the tele-phone wires and watch for the insects.

American kestrels are the most colorful of our predatory birds with their rufous backs and tails, light breasts, and black-streaked faces. The slate-blue wings of the males easily distinguish them from the females. In addition, the females are larger and more aggressive than the males. They often take the lead in courtship, and while they do most of the incu-bating of the eggs, the males are kept busy providing food for the females and their nestlings.

The nest is often nothing more than a deserted woodpeck-er hole or a natural cavity in a tree. No soft, insulating materi-al is used to cushion and warm the eggs. Our particular little family lives in a deserted pileated woodpecker nest in a power pole. Eventually, after a twenty-nine-day incubation period, three eggs hatched and for another month the nestlings stayed put. Then, in the beginning of July, they ventured out. That was when we first noticed the noise.

One ornithologist described an American kestrel as "an alert, noisy, suspicious bird whose incessant high-pitched alarm call becomes tiresome; it is especially noisy when a pair is escorting fledged young" (Bent, pt. 1, 248).

Its best-known call, "klee, klee," is used when it is excited, but we often heard a whining cry that is a food call. The "chitter," used by a pair when approaching each other, in display, copulation, and when feeding the young, is the most noise our own little family makes.

American kestrels may be small but they seem to be fearless. Many observers have reported their attacks on sharp-shinned and Cooper's hawks in defense of their territory or in an attempt to wrest food from the larger birds of prey. During a previous nesting on our mountain, back in 1979, Steve came in from the porch very excited. He had just watched the male American kestrel drive off a red-tailed hawk who had been hovering above some of the Muscovy ducklings we were raising at the time. It was Steve's belief that the aggressive presence of the kestrels was keeping our ducks safe from hawk predation. Certainly we did not lose any that summer to winged predators.

Although most American kestrels banded in Pennsylvania have been found in North Carolina, where they migrate in September and October, some, usually males, do not migrate. For several mild winters after the 1979 nesting I noticed a lone male sitting on the same power pole where the nest had been. I wondered if it was the same bird that had fathered our small family. I doubted it, because the life span of most American kestrels in the wild is only a year and a half. However, in captivity they live, on average, five years. Their chief enemy is humanity. More than 25 percent are killed by shooting and many more die from other humanity-related causes.

The late naturalist-anthropologist Loren Eiseley, in his book *The Immense Journey,* told of how as a young scientist he had been sent out to collect birds for a zoo. One night he captured a male American kestrel who had diverted Eiseley's attention from the female, who escaped. Something in Eiseley revolted against imprisoning such a spirited bird and the next morning, while building a cage for his captive, he whimsically released him.

As he flew high up into the air, Eiseley heard "from far up, a cry of unutterable and ecstatic joy," but it was not the male. The waiting female came hurtling down to greet her mate. "They met," Eiseley wrote, "in a great soaring gyre that turned to a whirling circle and a dance of wings. Once more, just once, their two voices joined in a harsh wild medley of question and response, then they were gone forever somewhere into those upper regions beyond the eyes of man" (191–92).

AUGUST 13. The woods still dripped from yesterday's rain. Mushrooms of all shapes and colors erupted from the ground, along with Indian pipes. The woods never smell sweeter than when they are wet. Shapes loom up in the mist and people the forest with all kinds of possibilities—both those creatures that I can still see here and those that have long been extirpated. Those ghosts often haunt me, the mountain lions, elk, wood buffaloes, and wolves that once roamed this mountain when it was a balanced ecosystem untouched by the meddling hands of humanity. Even Native Americans used our mountain lightly as a place to hunt but not inhabit. Today I must be content with a depauperate ecosystem of small predators and too many prey animals, an island surrounded by a sea of humanity pressing in on all sides.

Still, I have my moments when I can imagine myself to be alone in a wilderness observing the wild animals in a totally natural setting. Today, for instance, I was encircled by a chorus of scolding ovenbirds as I sat beneath my favorite black cherry tree. Suddenly the birds took off in every direction for no discernible reason. Next, an immature northern flicker landed silently on a tree limb above me for a look around. Then a gray squirrel harvested ripe wild black cherries high in the treetops, grabbing them with its front paws and shoving them into its mouth quickly while sitting on the branch on its haunches.

Returning along the First Field Trail, I encountered three half-grown raccoons walking up the trail toward me, digging in the grassy path as they moseyed along. I accidentally dropped a pencil, and they looked up, saw me, waddled over to a tree, and climbed up six feet. Then they lined up on the trunk, one directly above the next, to look at me. I remained still, which seemed to reassure them. Finally, they backed down to the ground, foraged a bit about the base of the tree, and walked off into the woods, swaying their behinds as they moved.

I walked a little farther down the trail and there were the raccoons again, off in the woods to my right, still foraging. When they saw me, two streaked at least thirty feet up a live tree. The other one ran up a broken-off trunk to its top (about ten feet) and sat there watching me. The two in the live tree headed back down the tree, this time head first, and once back on the ground, ambled over fallen trees, moving slowly and quietly away from me. Finally they disappeared from sight leaving the single coon on its own. It continued watching me, its eyes frightened, and so I left it in peace, confident that it would reunite with its siblings once I was gone.

AUGUST 14. Visibility was less than a hundred feet as I set out shortly after 8:00 A.M. and deer moved as silent wraiths in the mist. The woods dripped with fog. I was in a deciduous cloud forest festooned with spider artistry suspended from tree limbs and attached to stumps—an array of fish nets, diaphanous igloos, and other fantastic shapes, designed by a host of spiders of different species, some in evidence, others hidden.

An eastern wood pewee called along the Guesthouse Trail and a black-capped chickadee along Laurel Ridge Trail. When I sat on a hollow log, an ovenbird flew in, landed on a log four feet away, and called loudly. Soon it was joined by a second silent ovenbird. They foraged together in the shrubbery, the first one still calling loudly, its orange crest elevated. After several minutes they flew off, although I could hear occasional chips in the woods, probably from an assortment of birds on the move.

Along the Far Field Road, an adult wood thrush flew up from the underbrush, crossed the road, and started its quiet warning call. I spotted at least one immature thrush perched in a nearby tree. I sat down to watch and wood thrushes gathered around, across, and above me, some crying their quiet alarm, others silent and watchful. Trying hard not to move, I counted at least ten (and probably more) as they constantly shifted positions and tree perches, each time shaking the tree limbs as they landed, some even in the tree I was resting against. Only once did their quiet calls attract another species, a male hooded warbler who landed in a low tree branch five feet from me for a long, silent look before he flew off. Fog seems to do strange things to birds' perceptions of danger and their reactions to it. This weird chorus of wood thrushes lasted for at least ten minutes before they gradually dispersed.

First Field Trail was littered by a recent rain of fresh acorns. It is a great year for nuts and fruits, so the birds and animals will eat well this winter. Already cedar waxwings have arrived to harvest the wild black cherry crop. In the moisture, still more fresh Indian pipes had emerged from the soil along the Short Circuit Trail. On that same trail, one chickadee found me and started to scold. It was quickly joined by ten more for a few minutes, along with several warblers, but the latter didn't fly as close and in the fog I could not identify them. All I saw were flashes of yellow and gray, forerunners of fall migrants.

AUGUST 15. Humid with fog in the early morning after a 5:00 A.M. thunderstorm. An eastern wood pewee, Acadian flycatcher, and red-eyed vireo were the only singers this morning. The mosquitoes seemed to abate, the last couple of days, but the humid fog brought them out in force this morning.

To keep my sanity, I decided to find out more about mosquitoes. After all, forewarned is forearmed.

Mosquitoes probably evolved in the tropics at least two hundred million years ago and at first fed only on fruit juices and nectar. Both sexes still need such food for energy and other activities, but while the males, with no biting mouthparts for piercing the skin, eat only sugar-rich juice, the females only drink nectar before and after blood sucking.

Scientists think that female mosquitoes took up blood sucking when first the cold-blooded vertebrates evolved, followed by birds and mammals. Because blood contains valuable proteins that greatly increase egg production, it made sense for the egg-producing females to develop biting mouthparts so they could utilize the blood of other creatures.

As of 1991, scientists had discovered 3,450 species of mosquitoes with about eighteen new ones per year. Three-quarters of these species live in the tropics; some areas support as many as one hundred fifty species per square mile. Pennsylvania has about forty species, the United States as a whole one hundred seventy, Canada seventy, and the Arctic less than a dozen. The farther north you travel, the greater the density of mosquitoes. According to scientist Lewis T. Nielsen, "In the Arctic, thousands of square miles of tundra pools overlying permafrost produce hordes of mosquitoes that quite literally blacken the sky. In one experiment, Canadian researchers, who uncovered their torsos, arms, and legs to Arctic mosquitoes in the interests of science, reported as many as 9,000 bites per minute" (4).

Mosquitoes are the most dangerous creatures on earth to humans. As disease vectors they have killed more people than any other animal. For instance, one million infants a year die of mosquito-borne malaria in Africa. Mosquitoes also carry more than one hundred viral diseases to humans and other animals, including dengue, encephalitis, and yellow fever.

So what good are mosquitoes? They are important food for some birds and bats and the main pollinators of Arctic bog orchids and other wildflowers. Most never feed on humans. Those that do are called *anthropophilous,* which means "associated with humans." Most of our closest associates belong to the genus *Aedes,* which rest with their rear ends down when they feed on us.

Aedes vexans, which translates as "irritating pest," is the most common of several so-called floodwater mosquitoes that lay their eggs on dry land. The embryos of their eggs can remain dormant for many years until their eggs are immersed in water. In an Illinois woodland scientists discovered from 101 to 3,964 eggs in wooded depressions. Where soil absorbs and holds water because of detritus and shading by a low herbal canopy, such as our Laurel Ridge with its blueberry and laurel understory, the numbers of eggs were the highest. *Aedes vexans* also likes the walls of crayfish holes, which are abundant in our stream.

As eggs they provide food for mites, earthworms, ants, and beetles. As larvae swimming in their temporary pools they are choice food for salamanders and victims of both internal and external parasites. If they survive through four molts to pupate and finally hatch as adults, they live three weeks in the summer, feeding on plant nectar, particularly that of goldenrod. After mating, the female gets her blood meal. Altogether each generation lasts twenty-five to thirty days.

Other floodwater mosquitoes include *A. stimulans, punctor, excrucians, sticticus,* and *trivittatus,* and *Psorophora horida.* You don't need to know any Latin to get the general idea that these mosquitoes mean business.

AUGUST 16. Now insects call night and day while the molting songbirds quietly lie low. Cicadas almost drown out the persistent red-eyed vireos and the eastern wood pewees, the last of summer's avian singers and the most monotonous. Both epitomize lazy, hot, and humid summer days.

A couple of gray squirrels were still busy harvesting wild black cherries in the treetops, and on the ground I found a big pile of fresh bear scat filled with cherry pits.

The first smooth false foxglove (*Gerardia laevigata*) is blooming along the Laurel Ridge Trail. A member of the snapdragon family, its yellow, bell-shaped flowers especially prefer to grow along the edges of old mountain roads. Its genus name refers to John Gerard, fifteenth-century English botanist and the author of *Herball*. All members of this genus are thought to be parasitic on the roots of other plants.

Another parasite is the immigrant field plant butter-and-eggs or yellow toadflax (*Linaria vulgaris*). First introduced to America by a Welshman named Ranstead who planted it in his garden, probably for its supposed medicinal virtues, it has spread throughout the continent. Like smooth false foxglove, it is a member of the snapdragon family and sports yellow, snapdragonlike flowers with bright orange lips that must be pushed open by bumblebees to be pollinated. The orange mouth is thought to resemble that of a toad's so for centuries children have squeezed the blossom behind the lips to make the toad "talk." It has at least thirty common names including such puzzlers as "impudent lawyer" and "deadman's bones." Centuries ago its juice was mixed with milk to poison flies. Herbalists claimed it was able to cure such problems as jaundice, skin rashes, and hemorrhoids. Its flowers even produced a yellow dye.

White snakeroot (*Eupatorium rugosum*) is starting to open, lighting up the shadowy woods with its clusters of downy white blossoms, and in First Field the early goldenrod is already in full bloom.

AUGUST 17. Days of heat and humidity, but today I saw a little more action in the heat-stunned woods. A ruffed grouse flushed, deer ran off, and dozens of dragonflies coursed over the top of First Field, their gossamer wings shimmering in the sunlight. Then four American goldfinches sang from the top of the Norway spruces, and a ruby-throated hummingbird foraged at the trumpet creeper blossoms beside the driveway.

Best of all, though, was a high-hopping female wood frog, beige-pink in color, in the wet area along First Field Trail. Although I spend hours watching them court and mate in the spring at our tiny field pond, this is the first time I have ever seen an adult abroad in the summer. Once they leave the pond as tiny froglets, they are solitary creatures, preferring moist deciduous forests with a well-developed leaf litter. It takes two years for a male to sexually mature and three for a female, so the one I saw must have survived several years.

In the evening Steve went down to fish in the Little Juniata River at the base of our mountain. There he saw a great blue heron and a great egret as well as a huge snapping turtle and dozens of crayfish under the bridge that I often drive over, unaware of what lives in that watery world below. If the river were not squeezed between the railroad on one side and a busy highway on the other, I would spend time along its banks in search of the creatures that still live there. The fate, however, of the Melody Curtises of the world reminds me that as a woman it is safer to stay hidden away on a mountaintop where few humans go than to remain in plain view beside a busy highway.

AUGUST 18. David Quammen, in his book of witty nature essays, *Natural Acts,* written in 1985, makes it clear that he does not think much of butterflies. He calls them "the most vapidly prettified of all insects" and "an evolutionary experiment in sheer decorative excess" (47). More recently, scientific studies have proven how useful the "prettified" scales are to butterflies.

Two hundred million years ago, butterflies had both hairy

bodies and wings. Then spiders appeared on the evolutionary scene and found it easy to wrap those hairy-winged butterflies in their silken webs. So, according to Charles Remington of Yale University, mutants developed over time with flattened scales on their wings who were able to wriggle free from spider webs, leaving a few of the expendable scales behind. Scales, which are really modified hair cells attached to butterfly wings by tiny stalks, have other important functions. They are needed to provide wing lift. In some species of butterflies there are also scales on the males' wings that emit scent to attract females.

Butterflies need a body temperature of 80 degrees Fahrenheit to fly and so they sunbathe. During this activity, the scales either absorb the sun's heat and conduct it toward the butterfly's body or they reflect it directly onto the body. In either case, sunbathing can raise the butterfly's temperature more than 20 percent.

That is one reason why some butterfly species in our area, such as the spring azure, change their wing color from blue in the spring to white in the summer, since a darker color absorbs more heat.

Which brings us directly to the use of color in butterfly scales. Experiments show that while predators will frequently catch butterflies, once they get a closer look, they are often repelled by the bright patterns, particularly the eyespot decoration. Second, butterflies see color just as we do and so are able to recognize the color scheme of their own species during courtship.

So it turns out that Mr. Quammen's "decorative excess" is necessary for butterfly survival. Those of us who are butterfly lovers can continue to look forward to summer when butterflies, those "prismatic images of joy," as writer H. M. Tomlinson (124) once referred to them, turn our wildflower meadows brilliant with fluttering color as they did today.

AUGUST 19. About this time every summer people are fed up with insects. The clouds of mosquitoes and midges in wooded areas, the flies and ants in the dooryard, and the squash borers, striped cucumber beetles, and Mexican bean beetles attacking the garden seem to have us surrounded. In fact, we begin to believe that not only will the insects inherit the earth, but that they will do so by next week.

There are insects, however, that not only help us in our battle against the harmful ones, but that are also beautiful. Consider, for instance, the delicate lacewings with their large, golden eyes, pale green bodies, and gossamer wings. Another name for them—aphid lions—refers to their larval form when they prey on aphids as well as scale insects, mealy bugs, and whiteflies. These are all minuscule creatures that can wreak havoc in gardens and greenhouses.

Lacewings belong to the worldwide Chrysopidae family in the ancient insect order Neuroptera. In North America there are two common species that look alike. *Chrysoperla plorabunda* is the species found in our fields while *C. downesi* lives in coniferous forests. The females of both species lay up to six hundred single, pearlescent green, oval eggs on long, thin, silk-like stalks that they secrete from glands near the tip of their abdomens. These eggs hatch after a few days into larval aphid lions, eat voraciously through two molts, then spin cocoons and pupate.

C. downesi produces only one generation of offspring a summer, which spends the winter in the pupal stage, but *C. plorabunda* breeds continuously all summer, making them more valuable as pest killers, and only their last generation overwinters.

As adults, both species, like ants, eat the honeydew exuded by aphids and scale insects. To make up for such an unbalanced diet, they have yeast colonies living symbiotically in their digestive walls, which provide necessary amino acids for their vegetarian lifestyle.

Probably the most interesting part of the lacewings' life cycle is their courtship ritual. Sexually receptive lacewings of all species produce signals by vigorously vibrating their abdomens up and down in a rhythmic, repetitive manner, according to entomologist Charles S. Henry who has been studying them for several decades. Usually they do this on either a blade of grass or a leaf, which shakes with the vibrations and in that way passes the signal on for several inches.

Each lacewing species has its own distinctive series of vibrations, so only a lacewing of the same species will reply after hearing such signals through special receptors in its wings. *C. plorabunda's* song, for instance, is a string of repeated, identical volleys of vibrations. When a male and a female lacewing of the same species find each other, they touch mouthparts as they continue to vibrate and then they mate, staying coupled for as long as fifteen minutes.

Although adult lacewings are more active at night, with especially acute hearing in the ears located on their wings, today I found several clinging to grass stems in First Field.

AUGUST 20. Only a song sparrow sang at dawn. A little later a blue-headed vireo and an eastern wood pewee also sang, but mostly the dawn hours are quiet now after the deafening hubbub of katydids and their kin most of the night.

Along Laurel Ridge Trail a family of pileated woodpeckers shouted their demonic calls to one another. On the power line right-of-way a family of immature eastern towhees flushed. A deer skulked in the underbrush, watching me but not fleeing when I walked on.

A porcupine foraged on the ground above the Far Field Road bank. When it saw me it scooted or rather labored up a large white oak tree, moving first its front legs, then its back legs, and finally its tail in a slow, awkward climb. It was a small porcupine, probably newly on its own. Had I been a hunter, its inattention and then its inept ascent would have made it an easy target. It did not stop climbing, though, until it was high in the sheltering treetops.

As I emerged at the top of First Field, two birds flew off from the underbrush. I thought they were half-grown turkey poults but I was not certain until I neared First Field Trail and heard a hen turkey clucking. I looked around, thinking she was in the underbrush, but instead she flew off from the top of a tree. A second turkey flew off when I sat down beneath a tree at the top edge of First Field. Finally, walking back on the Short Circuit Trail, I found a fresh, large turkey feather in the middle of the trail, verifying my turkey sighting.

AUGUST 21. Sometime in April or early May, eastern box turtles emerge from the earth, where they hibernate from November onward, and begin anew their slow, easy, smart, and cautious lifestyle. Such traits have kept turtles going for two hundred million years. Eastern box turtles have further distinguished themselves as the longest-lived vertebrates in North America—up to 120 years of age for the few that have been positively marked and identified. Furthermore, they are the only fully terrestrial turtle in the eastern United States. They even mate on the ground, as I found out this beautiful August day.

As I walked along Laurel Ridge Trail, I heard a movement twenty feet off in the underbrush. At first I assumed it was the usual eastern towhee scratching around, but something about the sound seemed different. It was a pair of eastern box turtles in flagrante delicto under a blueberry shrub. The darker-colored, smaller female was right side up, and if turtles can look bored, she did. The male, on the other hand, was lying on his back, connected to her, tail end to tail end. His head was fully extended, his legs were waving around, and he looked like the turtle version of a gyrating Elvis.

They didn't seem in the least bit disturbed at my voyeurism, so I sat down and watched for about fifteen minutes.

Then I decided to risk going home for Bruce, hoping that he would be able to take some good photos of the mating. The turtles were still in the same positions when we returned about a half-hour later. While Bruce maneuvered into photographic position, I sat and continued watching. Flies buzzed about in the midday sunshine and, despite the dry weather, landed on us in hordes. Locusts trilled. Black-capped chickadees and eastern towhees called in the distance. Sunlight penetrated the green foliage and the wind blew with gentle clarity. Meanwhile, the turtles stayed under a sheltering blueberry shrub. Finally, the male disconnected, flailing with his legs, and flipped over as Bruce watched and photographed.

During the quarter of a century I have lived here I have had many close encounters with eastern box turtles, but that observation was my peak experience. Although an occasional wood turtle or snapping turtle appears near our stream, eastern box turtles are the most common turtles on the wooded ridges of our ridge-and-valley province. According to Larry L. Shaffer's *Pennsylvania Amphibians and Reptiles,* eastern box turtles are not found in the Allegheny Mountains but live in the southern two-thirds of the commonwealth in urban, suburban, and rural settings.

Eastern box turtles differ one from another in color and markings. Usually their carapaces or upper shells are dark brown or black with numerous irregular yellow, orange, or reddish spots, blotches, or stripes. Their plastrons or lower shells are also variable—yellow orange to tan—and their legs and heads can be a dull flesh color, yellow, or bright orange. Even their eye color varies according to their sex, with males having pink or bright red eyes, and females dark red, reddish brown, purple, or gray eyes.

Once eastern box turtles are out for the season, they spend much of their time in search of food. They are omnivorous and are especially fond of mushrooms (even the ones that are poisonous to us), mayapples, spiders, insects and their larvae, earthworms, slugs, snails, carrion, and fruits, especially berries.

Researcher Lucille F. Stickel tracked eastern box turtles over twenty-nine acres of the Patuxent Research Refuge in Laurel, Maryland, from 1944 to 1947. She discovered that they spend their nights in "forms" or cavities that they dig in the ground, sometimes constructing a new one every night, and other times reusing them for several nights. During unusually hot or cold weather or a drought, they may stay in their forms for days or weeks. Otherwise, when they are not eating, they sun themselves on gully banks, margins of grassy forest roads, and woodland openings formed by falling trees.

Mating is supposed to take place in spring, which is why I was amazed to discover the mating box turtles today, but apparently eastern box turtle females can store sperm for up to four years after their last mating. In addition, turtles do not synchronize the production of male sperm and female eggs. Instead, the male produces sperm in the fall and keeps it viable in his body throughout his winter hibernation.

As an inveterate box turtle watcher, I've discovered that they have different personalities. Some are shy, others are curious, still others aggressive. They have excellent eyesight, so it is difficult to surprise one. By sitting down beside each box turtle that I encounter and waiting, I have been able to watch them go about their reptilian business, heads held high, eyes alertly watching everything. In the slow silence of time we share, I feel as if I have taken a small step toward bridging the yawning gap between human and reptilian perception.

AUGUST 22. Just as the birds are leaving, so are Eva, Mark, and Luz. We put them on a plane to Austin, Texas, this afternoon and will not see them again until Christmas. Although Eva has not matured as fast as baby birds and mammals do, by the time she left she was trying to crawl. When next we visit her, the changes will be astounding as she continues her long, slow ascent to maturity. When she reaches young womanhood, I will be old, both of us a part of the inevitable earth cycle of birth, youth, maturity, old age, and death.

I spent many happy hours this summer carrying her around outside, showing her the wildflowers and grasses and the tree leaves waving in the breeze. We also "Rode a Cock-horse to Banbury Cross" and played "This Little Piggy," and I relearned all the extravagant voice and hand gestures that entertain little humans when they are bored.

We feel a little lost and sad now that she and her parents are gone. With her departure most of the summer is also gone. We are left with a pile of photos to post on the refrigerator and beside my computer and with memories that cannot be taken away from us. There will be other visits here over the years to come. Already her mother, although born and raised in the tropics, loves our Pennsylvania mountain. Even though Eva will not remember her first visit here, we hope that she will remember and cherish subsequent visits and that the mountain will become a favorite and safe destination during her lifetime.

AUGUST 23. On this cool, crystal-clear, and cloudless day, I took a walk over to the clear-cut along Greenbrier Trail, following the suggestion of a retired forester that I keep a record of the regrowth of the devastated area.

It was very wet and overgrown with grasses and blackberry canes. Gray catbirds, eastern towhees, and house wrens sang and called, while gray squirrels climbed over the bent and gnarled leftover trees. I also heard a singing red-eyed vireo and saw a black-and-white warbler, the latter in the wooded area between the two clear-cut zones. Black locust and striped maple saplings had sprung up in several areas along with red maple. The underbrush was thick and impenetrable, covering the naked scars of the clear-cut. Nature was filling a vacuum.

Hairy bush-clover, another new wildflower to the mountain and one that likes dry open places and roadsides, grew on the clear-cut knoll (Dogwood Knoll), now hot and sunny and covered with a blanket of grass, blackberry, low bush blueberry, and black locust. The scrubby, damaged trees had put out lots of leaves, and each was having its moment in the sun to dominate the knoll. Farther down the knoll, some striped maple and bracken fern were mixed in with a few red oak and more chestnut oak sprouts hidden in the underbrush here and there.

Ten Springs Trail (formerly the Lower Road), repeatedly scraped clean during the logging, still had many bare, stony areas. Elsewhere it was choked with blackberry canes. At the ruined wetland, where the logger had run his skidder and cut all the shading trees, I was pleased to find woolgrass (*Scirpus cyperinus*), a native, perennial bulrush.

Finally, I descended into the cool, green haven of the real forest in the deepest part of the hollow where eastern wood pewees called and stream water rippled over moss-covered ledges. I sat under a black gum tree beside a foot-high waterfall that made enough noise to drown out the mechanized sounds from the valley. Here I could again pretend that this forest was pristine and this mountain a wilderness untouched by the heavy hand of modern man.

AUGUST 24. Last summer, on this day, I sat along the Black Gum Trail watching deer file noisily past in the dry leaves. Then an ovenbird landed on a branch above me to pace back and forth and peer down at me in its intent way before flying off. The woods were mostly quiet, though, except for an occasional chipmunk.

When I continued my walk, I was suddenly stopped, almost in stupefaction, by the sight of three clumps of pine-sap—the first I had seen anywhere on the mountain since the appearance of sixty-three plants in 1984 and a couple of dozen less in 1985 halfway up Guesthouse Trail (see *Appalachian Autumn*, 26–28). Those plants were at least a half-mile from the first site and had certainly not been there before. What mysterious plants they are, appearing like ghosts in another place so long after the first ones, and the first ones never (so far) reappearing. More goes on beneath the soil than we can ever dream of.

Today I took the same walk and found not a sign of pine-saps.

AUGUST 25. Bruce and I celebrated our thirty-fourth wedding anniversary this beautiful, warm, moonlit night by skulking around outside with a flashlight, trying to find the insect choristers of the evening.

The most noticeable and loudest of all the songs came from the treetops, a surging "waa-waa" sound that made it difficult to hear the other noises of the night. We could not locate any of the insects without climbing the trees, but we were certain the songsters were male snowy tree crickets.

These crickets are well-known for their ability to accurately record the temperature since the frequency of their calls varies with the warmth of the night. The temperature can be figured by counting the number of chirps in thirteen seconds and then adding forty to the total to get the number of degrees Fahrenheit.

Crickets and katydids, members of the insect order Orthoptera along with mantids, walking sticks, grasshoppers, and cockroaches, are the principal evening singers. They produce their calls by drawing the scraper on one front wing cover over the filelike device on the other front wing. This process is called stridulation.

Most of the calls are produced exclusively by the male to attract the female for mating purposes, but male tree crickets have a further refinement. When they raise their wings to sing, they expose a gland that secretes an odoriferous liquid that is attractive to females. The latter climb onto the backs of the males to drink the liquid and then they mate at the same time.

During our search, we heard six different songs, indicating the presence of at least six separate species of crickets, grasshoppers, and katydids. Many look quite similar and for a long time all North American field crickets, for instance, were believed to be the same species.

One entomologist was not convinced, and his subsequent research uncovered six species of field crickets alone, which look almost identical. However, they would not interbreed. After much study, the only major difference scientists could find was in their songs, which varied from species to species.

We walked along, trying to track down the songsters, but we could rarely find them despite our flashlights. Finally, Bruce located a cone-headed grasshopper, one of the long-horned grasshopper family Tettigoniidae, clinging to a long blade of grass in First Field. He was the same green color as the grass and more than an inch in length. His long, red, hair-like antennae waved as his wings pulsated.

How many times do the various songsters call? Scientists estimate that a single green katydid rasps its wings together from thirty to fifty million times each season, while the naturalist Edwin Way Teale in his book *Near Horizons* calculates that snowy tree crickets "scrape wing against wing as many as 10,000 times on a summer night of average warmth" (76).

Once we were out looking for singers, we made other discoveries about night creatures as well. Along the road we found the larvae of lightning bugs that scavenge among the debris and emit an intermittent glow, the reason for their nickname "glowworms." They are easy to see with flashlights—flat, brown, six-legged creatures—but they were most attractive in the dark. Sometimes there were so many that we seemed to be walking among stars that had fallen to earth.

We are not often abroad at night and once, while I was searching for crickets that were calling from somewhere within the guest house stone wall, I heard the snorting of several deer. They had evidently been drinking from the drainage ditch at the base of the front lawn. Apparently I had disturbed their nightly 11:00 P.M. ritual, so they continued snorting in protest as they bounded off into the woods.

We also heard, periodically, an eastern screech owl calling from somewhere on Sapsucker Ridge.

Despite other distractions, we kept ourselves focused on the insect chorus, feeling, as cricket admirer H. A. Allard once said, according to Howard Ensign Evans in *Life on a Little Known Planet,* "better, broader, wiser, happier for having heard the crickets and katydids, for somehow they are points of kinship in our lives, even though our magnitudes and roles of living seem so far apart" (101).

AUGUST 26. Humid and warming up rapidly, so I took a quick, sweaty walk besieged by mosquitoes in the early morning. Northern flickers foraged on the Short Way Trail. Eastern wood pewees and blue-headed vireos were the only bird singers. A flock of black-capped chickadees foraged along the power line right-of-way, accompanied by common yellow-throats and eastern towhees.

The trails were green tunnels that filtered the fierce sunlight and provided a balm to my heat-weary body. The moss cushioned my footfalls. Above the green canopy, the sky burned a hot, steely blue, cloudless and hazy, essence of deep summer.

During the blistering hot days of summer, I make as many adjustments in my daily schedule as I do in winter's deepest cold. I get up and out early for my walk, dressed in light, baggy cotton pants and tank top. I close the windows and pull the shades to trap in the night's coolness before the sun rises. I eat cold soups and salads. Nothing hot goes into my stomach except in the cool, breakfast hours. I exercise in front of the fan in the briefest of outfits; I work in my upstairs study only until early afternoon.

Then I move down to the living room, the coolest room in the house, and turn on the ceiling fan. I both write and read away the hottest afternoon hours, sipping glasses of iced tea. In the evening, I throw up the windows and sometimes take a short walk. Once the sun sets, I sit on the veranda and enjoy the cooling temperatures. In my bedroom, the hottest room in the house, a fan blows all night long, pulling in enough cool air to make it comfortable under a light sheet.

By adjusting my schedule and not fighting the heat, I manage to survive, indeed thrive, during a heat wave. Just as a cold spell in deep winter does, a heat wave forces me into a more contemplative mood, slows me down, and gives me an excuse to be instead of do.

AUGUST 27. Overnight the humidity dropped, leaving us with a clear, cool morning. A large flock of birds appeared in the yard at seven—tufted titmice and black-capped chickadees accompanied by migrating warblers including a Canada and several black-and-white warblers. Where has the summer gone? Already the yellowing black walnut leaves are drifting down.

A large slimy salamander was stretched out this morning on the bottom step of the outside cellar stairs. What was it doing in such a barren environment and where had it come from? Slimy salamanders do like a wide variety of terrestrial habitats—moist ravines, shale banks, flood plains, cave entrances, beneath leaf piles—but a concrete cellar stair? Despite its propensity to exude a whitish secretion when handled that sticks like glue for days afterwards, after asking it what it was doing there, I picked up the attractive white-speckled black salamander and put it in the herb garden where it quickly disappeared. Perhaps it knew I was merely a good Samaritan because it did not leave a bit of slime on me; or maybe it sensed that I am a salamander lover.

I found a single pinesap blooming along Laurel Ridge Trail, more than a mile from where I found last year's clump and nearly half a mile from the bonanza eleven years ago. As usual, there is not a coniferous tree in sight even though pinesap is supposed to prefer coniferous forests, especially the pine and spruce forests of northern Europe. In fact, its species' name *hypopithys* means "under a pine or fir."

Two American copper butterflies mated at the Far Field, which is now yellow with opening goldenrod of several species, a welcome larder to a wide variety of nectar-loving and -pollinating insects.

A second pile of bear scat appeared along the Sapsucker Ridge Trail and it, like the other pile, was filled with cherry pits. I heard the steady plopping of falling cherries as I sat in Sapsucker Ridge woods and the keening cries of foraging cedar waxwings.

Silverrod, the only white goldenrod, bloomed at the top of First Field. Otherwise, waves of goldenrod billowed across First Field and fluttered with butterflies, chiefly monarchs, silver-spotted skippers, alfalfas, and cabbages.

At night I lay awake listening to the loud and persistent katydids, the swan song of summer. It seemed as if their pulsing calls should be lifting and rocking the house with their cadence. Much later, a nearby eastern screech owl added its trills to the katydid cacophony.

AUGUST 28. I walked over to the clear-cut on Greenbrier Trail and ran into flocks of migrating birds including many warblers, some of which I did pish down close enough to identify. Lots of eastern towhees fed on wild grapes. So did a northern cardinal. A ruby-throated hummingbird landed on a branch in front of me, along with a common yellowthroat.

The air seemed filled with birds as I walked along. I spotted an immature hairy woodpecker and a female American redstart, but most of the birds were frustrating flashes across the sky or among the leaf-covered trees. Still, it was a great day for birds if not for one middle-aged birdwatcher with slow reactions, bad eyes, and poor binoculars.

The action was just as frantic along Ten Springs Trail. Altogether I identified thirty-six species including an immature Wilson's warbler, a worm-eating warbler, magnolia warbler, black-and-white warbler, Nashville warbler, and chestnut-sided warbler, all heading south ahead of autumn's coming chill. How little time they have been here and already they are leaving.

AUGUST 29. At last the mosquito scourge is diminishing. I was actually able to stop on Laurel Ridge Trail, pish in a black-throated blue warbler, and watch a gray squirrel foraging for acorns in an oak tree without being besieged by mosquitoes. With that encouragement, I worked my way down to the Far Field thicket, overgrown with the wildflowers Pennsylvania smartweed and beggar ticks, also known as sticktights. I was in quest of blooming Hercules' club trees. Instead, all I found were dead snags. Not one tree had a trace of greenery. Apparently the debarking by hungry deer in the winter had killed them.

Finally I am reconnecting to a slower pace of life after the bustle of visitors for three months. Although signs of change are in the air, I am still in a summer woods, shrouded in green. Behind its screening leaves, a hidden world exists that I see only dimly.

I took a midafternoon walk through the monarch butter-fly–studded First Field, then down past Margaret's place to the bridge where I flipped a few rocks in search of salamanders. I saw two that moved so fast I barely had a glimpse of them before they disappeared into the wet soil. I need quicker, younger hands and eyes than I have to catch and identify them.

Along the road white wood asters, turtleheads, and beechdrops bloomed while the yellow blossoms of horse balm had already faded, but when I ran my fingers over the spent blossoms, I could still smell their odor of fresh lemons.

AUGUST 30. I sensed a magic to this thirtieth day of August. A high-pressure system has blown in over the mountain, and my early morning walk was pleasant and cool. I was able to move quietly, stopping to investigate a rustling in the bushes that meant a gray squirrel, pausing as a chipmunk skittered up the path ahead of me, and admiring a pair of common yellowthroats as they foraged among the scrub oaks.

There was nothing special about what I had seen so far, until I reached the Far Field. Bruce had cut it with our Bushhog two weeks ago, carefully trimming around two cool copses of locust and red maple trees and creating several narrow, grassy passageways between copses and woods.

This is not a farmer's field, but a naturalist's laboratory and, as I soon discovered, a play yard for deer.

I walked across the top of the field, heading for the entrance to the Sapsucker Ridge Trail, when suddenly I spotted deer running across an open patch at the other end of the Far Field beyond the second locust copse, about 260 feet away from me. At first I thought they were running because they saw me, but nevertheless I froze into place. The deer made quick, sharp turns and raced back the length of the narrow strip.

I realized that they had not seen me; they were playing. It looked like a family—a large doe, two smaller yearling does, and a fawn that was just losing its spots. The older sisters seemed to be teaching their smaller sibling how to play, bouncing about the youngster with exuberant energy. Even the mother joined in, although she was more sedate.

As part of her vigilance, the mother glanced up at my end of the field. I had not moved, but I was certain that my shape stood out against the newly mown field. The breeze blew in my face, so she could not catch my scent. However, she was clearly bothered at something she could not account for.

At first the others continued their play as the mother watched me. Then one of the yearlings joined her in looking. The other yearling and the fawn ran at breakneck speed into the woods and emerged on the other side of the second locust copse, seventy-five feet closer to me. The mother and first yearling quickly joined them.

Then they were all looking at me and advanced four abreast to within one hundred feet of where I was standing. The mother began to stomp first one front leg, then the other, in warning, but the fawn, trusting to its mother's judgment no doubt, calmly spread its back legs and attended to the call of nature.

She waited until her fawn finished and then she continued to stomp as she again moved forward, accompanied by her offspring. There was no menace in their advance. They merely looked like extremely nearsighted people peering curiously at me. I felt a mounting excitement in the silent ballet, and I wondered how close they would come.

Finally, at a distance of eighty feet, they all stopped and the mother snorted explosively. I had heard the sound many times, but it never fails to startle me. She snorted again, and they retreated back to one hundred twenty feet. There were more restless looks, and a little nervous feeding. At last the mother made up her mind. Snorting loudly, she was off with her children in close pursuit, and I was left alone in the field.

AUGUST 31. I pished up three red-eyed vireos along Laurel Ridge Trail feeding under the leaves of two scrawny cucumber magnolia trees. Although one grows on either side of the trail, I had never noticed them before until the vireos drew my attention to them, perhaps because I did not expect them to be growing on top of the dry ridge surrounded by chestnut oak trees, but down in the moist hollow where many stately ones live.

Then I spotted a black bear lumbering down the trail toward me. When I tried to step quietly off the trail to give him room, he heard my feet crackle in the dry leaves, looked up, saw me, hesitated, and finally ran back up the trail almost out of sight before pausing for a few seconds as if reluctant to change his direction. Then he disappeared.

A steady plopping of shells, like raindrops, alerted me that the two shagbark hickory trees above the Far Field Road were being harvested by what sounded like a platoon of squirrels. It was hard to spot the animals, but I did see a fox squirrel rapidly shelling the nuts from an exposed branch. Even though I was sitting two feet away from the nearest hickory tree branches, occasional pieces of shell hit me. Every minute or so a whole nut fell with a thud. There was not a sound from the squirrels except for the gnawing of teeth.

Later, lying against a pit mound (a mound of dirt from a large, uprooted tree), I spent a couple of hours watching and listening, not only to the squirrels but to a singing black-and-white warbler, a blue-gray gnatcatcher, flocks of American robins, cedar waxwings, eastern towhees, and a pair of pileated woodpeckers. I lay so still that the squirrels did not know I was there and neither did a still-spotted fawn that grazed within five feet of where I was. Finally it disappeared behind the mound, but when I started suddenly at a loud thud from a nearby tree, the fawn looked up, bounded off a short distance, stamped its front hoof, and then ran away snorting.

This, of course, set off the squirrels. I was no longer invisible to them. They started scolding. Then two young gray squirrels, judging from their thin tails, eased themselves down nearby tree trunks, their bodies and tails pressed flat against the trees, alertly watching me all the while. I remained still, which seemed to reassure them, so they scampered back up into the tree.

I was almost certain they had been sent by the others to check me out. Both seemed to communicate with their fellow squirrels in some silent manner, because the scolding slowly died away and all the squirrels resumed eating. One of the spy squirrels even sat visibly out on a limb and groomed itself.

At last I stood up to continue my walk, expecting a further outburst of scolding. The squirrels ignored me. Apparently I had been accepted—at least for the day—as an odd but harmless presence.

September

As imperceptibly as grief
The summer lapsed away,—
Too imperceptible, at last,
To feel like perfidy.

Emily Dickinson

 SEPTEMBER 1. Two deer were in the backyard this morning, one mostly brown except for a bit of gray on her neck, the other already wearing her gray back of fall and winter but still retaining her brown summer underparts. At the bottom of the driveway, I stood and watched as a doe grazed along the Short Circuit Trail. She ambled right up to within fifteen feet of me, stopped to look me in the eye for several seconds, and then turned calmly aside to continue her grazing along the edge of the road.

Chimney swifts twittered over the ridge top, beginning their fall migration. I explored Laurel Ridge, down below the Lady Slipper Trail, with Bruce this morning. Eastern wood pewees still called. Otherwise I heard an occasional flock of American goldfinches, a northern cardinal, Carolina wren, pileated woodpecker, and eastern chipmunk. We followed a labyrinth of deer trails etched into the mountainside through an understory of blueberry shrubs, bracken fern, and mountain laurel most of the way down the ridge until within a hundred feet of the stream. There a solid wall of green screened the view across to Sapsucker Ridge. It is a summer woods still, but heading into autumn as bird song fades and the daylight dwindles.

Eating lunch on the veranda, we were vastly entertained by watching an iridescent blue spider wasp hauling a spider larger than itself along the veranda and around into the grass at the side of the house. Later in the afternoon, David noticed it hauling another, which it dropped, and then returned to and dragged away, pulling it down into a deep hole dug in our window well. Spider wasps of the family Pompilidae prey only on spiders. Usually they immobilize them with a sting before hauling them off to their burrow in the ground where they or their larvae can feed on the still-living spiders at their leisure.

SEPTEMBER 2. We've been blessed by a Canadian high that slowly lowered the temperature to fifty-two degrees this morning, producing autumnal weather of clear blue skies, fluffy clouds, and a breeze. Along Greenbrier Trail I heard gray catbirds and eastern wood pewees and pished up common yellowthroats and other immatures I couldn't identify. Turkey vultures wheeled overhead and a ruffed grouse "putputted." I also found a steaming pile of fresh bear dung colored purple with whole corn kernels studding the amorphous mass.

Along the ridge top trail I pished up hooded warblers and heard cedar waxwings calling. American robins and eastern towhees were abundant. Red-bellied and hairy woodpeckers called, and flocks of red-eyed vireos moved through.

Best of all, though, was the view I had of a large fox squirrel scolding from the branch of a big chestnut oak tree studded with fat acorns. Its scolding is much more explosive than that of the gray squirrel and its tail fluffy and long enough to curl over its head like a fashionable parasol. At one point the squirrel hung over a smaller limb so that I could see its scrotum and identify it as a male. Finally his scolding wound down and he climbed back up to a topmost branch to resume eating acorns. Each time he would pick a nut and then retreat down to a lower, stronger limb to eat it. There he would sit, holding the acorn between his paws and revolving it like an ear of corn as he shelled and ate it. He repeated this routine several times and no doubt continued after I continued on my walk.

Later, walking along Laurel Ridge Trail, I spotted a question mark butterfly feeding on a wet area (probably sap) on a chestnut oak tree. *Polygonia interrogationis* had its winter coloration already. A large, orange and black butterfly, its hind wing is mostly black with short, taillike projections in the summer, but in fall and winter it is orange and black with longer, violet-tipped projections. It is named for the pearly silver question mark on the underside of its hind wing, which remains the same all year long. Like other anglewings (butterflies whose wing edges are irregularly shaped), question mark adults live in wooded areas and feed on rotting fruit, sap flows, or animal dung. All anglewings overwinter as adults, but question marks and hop merchants migrate south in the fall and return in the spring. No doubt this one was in the midst of migration.

SEPTEMBER 3. Lots of acorns lie on the ground already, and the woods rustled with foraging squirrels and chipmunks. I sat in the middle of Laurel Ridge Trail as a chipmunk scampered into view. It climbed onto a fallen branch to clean its front paws and face. Then it moseyed toward me looking for food. As it climbed up to a fallen limb, it suddenly saw me sitting three feet away. It emitted a shriek and ran back to the other fallen branch where it sat clucking loudly, its cheeks vibrating with every call, its twitching tail over its back. After several minutes, it sat up on its haunches and quietly called, almost like a whisper. Then it ceased altogether and just looked at me writing notes, as a few beams of weak sunlight filtered through the leaves and an eastern wood pewee called.

The wild mushrooms this year continue to be varied and beautiful. A beige-white one shone like mother-of-pearl. Bright orange mushrooms rimmed with yellow grew on fallen logs. One was lighter than the rest and striated with dark and light orange. There were small purple, yellow, and red cups, every imaginable shade of brown and beige, urn-shaped black mushrooms, and more mother-of-pearl, this time with grayish-purple and beige overtones as well as white. Clumps of orange fingers grew on the Sapsucker Ridge Trail.

Mushrooms, which are neither plants nor animals, are the reproductive structures or fruiting bodies of fungi. Most commonly they have colorful caps, gills, and stalks that brighten our woods floor with every imaginable color from late August until the end of October. Those capped mushrooms range from dinner plate size to pinheads. Some have ruffled edges, others the squat look of a child's drawing. Trying to identify many of them using standard mushroom guides is nearly impossible.

This is a great year for stinkhorns, the easiest of mushrooms to identify. In the Far Field woods I found some growing on the forest floor while others erupted on a rotting log. One even pushed its way up through the bark. Dozens and dozens of stinkhorns in all stages of development and decay spread over about two square yards.

The stinkhorns varied in color. Some had pale pink stalks, brown caps, and pinkish tips. They were *Mutinus caninus* or common stinkhorns. Others sported white stalks with grayish-green caps and are called stinkhorns, *Phallus ravenelii*. All bore an amusing resemblance to the human organ that the latter's genus name suggests.

Although most mushrooms produce spores on the outside of microscopic club-shaped cells called "basidia," stinkhorn mushrooms are related to puffballs, earthstars, dead man's fingers, and bird's nest mushrooms, which produce spores inside microscopic saclike mother cells called "asci." Incidentally, unlike the generic-shaped mushroom species, all are easy to identify.

Those asci cells of stinkhorns develop in an egg-shaped sac that elongates and ruptures within a three-hour time span when the stinkhorn matures. The egg sac remains at the base of the hollow, stalklike elongation as a volva or tissue that surrounds the developing mushroom, while a slimy layer containing the spores covers the top of the stinkhorn. That layer is also stinky, hence the common name, but the odor attracts insects that walk over the sticky spores and then distribute them wherever they next land.

Mushrooms, as David Aurora, author of *Mushrooms Demystified,* writes, are "nature's recyclers, the soil's replenishers." Each fruiting body is sustained by miles of microscopic filaments, called hyphae, which snake through the forest floor and into rotting logs, secreting enzymes that break down complex carbohydrates into the nutritive sugars needed by the mushroom. They also break down woody materials into forest soil. By feeding on dead and living matter, fungi break it down so it can be reused by plants.

With such understanding of what mushrooms do, we've come a long way from ancient peoples who did not understand how mushrooms grew and, not surprisingly, called them "a callosity of the earth," "earthy excrescences," and "the evil ferment of the earth." According to David T. Jenkins, the Roman naturalist Pliny believed that "the origin of mushrooms is the slime and souring juices of moist earth, or frequently the root of acorn-bearing trees; at first it's flimsier than froth, then it grows substantial like parchment, and then the mushroom is born."

As more and more information about the life cycles of mushrooms is uncovered by scientists, the truth about their life history is even stranger than the fiction.

SEPTEMBER 4. After the comparative quiet of August, the birds were revitalized today. Suddenly the woods were almost as busy with birds—both residents and migrants—as they had been in May and June. Black-capped chickadees, white-breasted nuthatches, and tufted titmice, followed by Blackburnian, black-throated green, and black-and-white warblers, foraged in our black walnut trees. Already the black walnut leaves are turning and falling like yellow confetti in the slightest breeze, making it easier to watch the flashes of color that signify migrating warblers.

By eight this morning I was heading across the goldenrod-covered First Field, which was flapping with dozens of migrating monarch butterflies. The sun sent beams down through the slight mist like a blessing on the field and woods and caught the dew that sparkled on every grass blade and tree leaf. Crickets and grasshoppers called from the depths of the field grasses. Orb webs, strung between goldenrod plants, shimmered in the sunlight.

In Margaret's Woods the understory glowed with white snakeroot. A deer snorted and four leaped up from where they had been bedded down. A red-eyed vireo droned on and on, a monotonous contrast to the brief "chewinks" of eastern towhees.

Along Greenbrier Trail the trees fluttered with calling and singing birds. There were more black-and-white and black-throated green warblers as well as magnolia and golden-winged warblers, common yellowthroats, and ovenbirds. Northern flickers, pileated woodpeckers, American robins, and eastern wood pewees called, and gray catbirds scolded while a northern cardinal, scarlet tanager, and chestnut-sided warbler sang. A dozen ruffed grouse erupted from beneath an overladen elderberry bush, purple with berry clusters. Once I flushed four yellow and green scarlet tanagers from the underbrush. They were probably immatures, the males not due to don their black and red coat until next spring. As I sat under my favorite white oak tree on Dogwood Knoll, I heard the tin drum call of a red-breasted nuthatch.

I walked for hours, distilling the essence of summer's impending end. At night I listened as eastern screech owls and great horned owls cried counterpoint to the pulsating calls of katydids.

SEPTEMBER 5. The golden light of dawn slid down the hillside toward me as I sat on the veranda watching the sunlight illuminate the waves of goldenrod spreading across First Field. A pair of common yellowthroats foraged in the lilac bush beside me. A house wren scolded; but mostly the late summer dawn was silent after the long, loud night of insect music.

The First Field goldenrod was covered with monarch butterflies, occasional alfalfas, and a meadow fritillary. I watched a pair of monarchs mating, abdomen to abdomen, on a goldenrod flower. Then they flew off, still connected, high into the air. They were looking for a patch of dense vegetation where they will remain from two to fourteen hours while the male transfers his packet of sperm to the female.

I continued my walk along Greenbrier Trail, but not much seemed to be abroad until I laid down against a bank to rest. Then gray catbirds, blue jays, eastern towhees, and American robins called. A distant woodpecker performed a drum roll, a pileated yelled, and finally a gray squirrel ascended a nearby hickory tree to harvest the nuts. Sitting quietly in the woods and being alert to all that goes on around me can be rewarding, especially if I use my ears as well as my eyes.

As I descended into the hollow, the dry leaves crackled under my feet, sending two ruffed grouse and several chipmunks off in a panic. An unseen bird of prey, probably a red-tailed hawk, screamed its rage over and over, but I never saw it, hidden, as it was, by the curtain of green leaves that still clothes the forest trees.

Walking up the road I glimpsed at least six wild turkeys foraging along the stream, and they fled in all directions when they saw me.

SEPTEMBER 6. Hurricane Fran slammed into the Carolinas last night and is moving toward us. It has been downgraded to a tropical storm, but it is still expected to hit us with heavy wind and rain. The birds were active, and I pished in a mixed flock of black-capped chickadees, eastern wood pewees, black-throated blue warblers, and others that zipped silently back and forth, high in the treetops and impossible to see with all the leaves on the trees. The woods were dark and blustery with the look only an imminent hurricane-engendered storm can give them.

An immature red-tailed hawk played in the winds of First Field, looking as if it enjoyed the power of its wings pitted against gusts that sent it soaring upward.

A feeling of expectation settled over the woods and fields, and the humid air held the promise and threat of the coming deluge. Two does trotted quickly along the edge of First Field. A flock of blackbirds swirled over the power line right-of-way and settled into the trees. Bumblebees clung to the swaying goldenrod as they continued to gather nectar and pollen. A bare black walnut limb overhanging the driveway started to gather up monarchs; first five, and then I watched as the sixth one sailed in. All clung to a branch as if prepared to ride out the storm on swaying branches instead of hidden in the depths of First Field beneath the goldenrod. A common yellowthroat scolded from the garage forsythia bush.

The rain started at 2:30 P.M., and by the time Bruce arrived home at 5:30, the wind had increased to fifty miles an hour, pruning trees of limbs and leaves. One loud crack was a portion of a backyard black locust splitting off. A tinkle of glass and I found that my antique, rose-colored, glass vase on the mantelpiece had been shattered by wind that threw rain across our front porch and through the open door. Then the rain suddenly increased to tumultuous volume, beating against the bow window so hard that it leaked, spattering the desk. Bruce ran out to open some of the road grates, already jammed with debris, and prepared to spend the night downstairs on the couch so he could rush out whenever the rain increased to try to save the road. Luckily, though, the rain diminished after two hard downbursts, but in the middle of the night we lost our electricity for nearly three hours.

SEPTEMBER 7. Off and on rain today. The damage to the road was minimal. Two trees were down, which Bruce cleared, along with numerous branches. To our relief, the ditches and drains worked well in the hollow and there was a minimum of washing so the road held. I walked down to the forks in the morning to look at the rushing stream, a sight I rarely see in late summer.

A misty rain, which barely penetrated the forest cover, had continued into midafternoon as I walked my usual circuit over the moss-covered trails of Laurel Ridge, the Far Field Road, and Sapsucker Ridge Trail. The trails were littered with small and a few large chestnut oak branches, all heavily laden with clusters of attractive acorns. One small branch held twenty-two by actual count. I assume that the weight made them top-heavy and easily whipped off by the wind, just as my rose vase, made top-heavy by dried flowers, was overturned by the wind.

I found a dead young male gray squirrel lying on his back on the Far Field Road, presumably inexperienced in such a storm and swept to his death. White snakeroot and goldenrod were beaten to the ground in many places. The natural and human world appeared chastened by the fury of a storm that none of us could control, a trump card nature still has over the arrogance of humanity. We can trash the earth's forests and prairies, pave it over, mine its depths, drive wildlife and plants to extinction, but we still can't do much about the weather.

An eastern wood pewee called. Ruffed grouse erupted like miniature helicopters from the edge of the Sapsucker Ridge Trail. No doubt they were after the wild black cherries littering the ground. An uprooted red maple tree had fallen across the trail. Farther along, at the edge of First Field, a nest of fallen red maple trees and branches blocked the way. Black locusts were also uprooted in that corner of First Field. It looked as if an unusually hard blast of wind had hit the area in a swath that extended down the hillside to the edge of the Far Field Road. The Norway spruces were silver with mist and rain but untouched by the storm. Cedar waxwings and a mourning dove called from the depths of the spruce grove.

SEPTEMBER 8. As I walked the Black Gum Trail, I spotted a woodchuck. Sensing a problem (me), it stood up on its hind legs, its front paws clasped piously across its belly, and peered around, but I never moved. Finally it slowly made its way up the hill, pausing frequently to look in my direction and twice popping up from behind a fallen log as if to catch me moving. I'm always pleased to come across a woodchuck in the woods, its natural habitat before humans altered the landscape, instead of in the lawn and fields where most prefer to live so they can dine on our vegetables and flowers and undermine the foundations of our houses and other buildings with their den holes. The woodchuck in such a habitat seems like a parasite, the woodchuck in the woods a free agent.

Descending to the road on Pit Mound Trail, I walked up the road to look at the still heavily flowing stream and at all the wildflowers in bloom—turtlehead and beechdrops, silver-

rod and white wood asters. Near the guest house a pearl crescent butterfly foraged on the vibrantly colored wavy-leaved
asters.

Later, David reported a new wildflower growing on top of
the old farm dump we closed nineteen years ago. It is slowly
being reclaimed by nature although the dregs of old tires and
broken furniture are still discernible beneath the patina of
green that covers it. For years white snakeroot has persisted
amid the broken bottles and discarded soup cans, but the center of the dump now features five-foot-high, yellow ironweed
or wingstem (*Actinomeris alternifolia*). Dressed in white and
gold, the abandoned dump looks almost presentable to my
critical eyes. At least I no longer avert them when I walk past.

SEPTEMBER 9. This morning I had another close encounter with a handsome fox squirrel, this time along the Far
Field Road. Using my voice and the same tone I had with
Eva, I kept the squirrel at eye level on a nearby tree, its legs
splayed out, its bushy red tail flopped over its head so that the
tail's black-edged, red underside was displayed. At first the
squirrel nervously flicked its tail as I talked, but finally it re-
laxed enough to descend the tree, climb over a fallen tree
limb, then down to the ground, across the road in front of
me, and into the woods on the other side. The last I saw, it
had climbed up a large oak tree and was hidden by the leaf
cover.

Two years ago I discovered a single nodding ladies' tresses
along the edge of the Far Field, forty feet below the enclosure
David built to protect our round-leaved orchid. I could hard-
ly believe the coincidence. As I walked on I found a second
plant forty feet from the first, still at the edge of the Far Field,
and a third one nearby that had already finished blooming.
With grasslike leaves at the base of its stem and small, white,
bell-shaped flowers twisting up its stem, this is one of the
less showy wild orchids. Still, it was a satisfying discovery.

Last year the same three plants bloomed in the same location.

Today I searched again for nodding ladies' tresses. First I found a single plant still in bud. Then, a few feet beyond, I spotted a lovely cluster of sixteen opening plants. What an encouraging increase from the last two years.

Coming back along the Short Circuit Trail, I encountered thirteen pinesaps in bloom. A second plant had also joined the first one I found on Laurel Ridge Trail several days ago. How many more will I find this year? We tend to think of wildflowers as immobile, but pinesap and pink lady's slippers, to give only a few examples, are almost as active as some mammals.

SEPTEMBER 10. An ovenbird flushed along the Far Field Road. Asters were blooming at the Far Field. Large numbers of both monarch and cabbage white butterflies foraged in the goldenrod fields. It seems to be an excellent year for migrating monarchs. On some days I've counted close to a hundred fluttering over our fields, heading determinedly south on what seem to be frail wings.

I pished a black-throated green warbler within a few feet of where I was standing on the Short Circuit Trail. Then a fawn leaped almost directly in front of me while its more cautious mother circled widely. A long, slender, yellow coral fungus *Clavariadelphus ligula* that prefers to live in conifer duff grew on the trail near yesterday's pinesap discovery.

A yellow and black spider with rusty-red legs was deftly spinning its web across Short Way Trail. It frequently dropped down invisible lines like a trapeze artist or twisted its body up and down visible lines as if it were knitting with its body. It repeatedly returned to the web's whitened center from which all the guy lines were being spun. A yard-and-a-half line ran to a sapling at the edge of the trail; another reached up a foot and a half to a leaf from an overhanging tree branch. Others radiated out like spokes in a wheel. All the while I watched it work, it ignored me, or, more likely, did not know that I was there. In its world, I was too big to be prey or predator.

At dusk, a parade of bats fluttered over the house as I sat on the veranda. Whether they were only a few bats continually circling over the house or a steady procession of new bats I couldn't tell, but it was wonderful to watch their silent progression. Silent to us, but of course they were communicating by echolocation—high-frequency sounds that humans can't hear.

SEPTEMBER 11. On this cool, windy, and clear day there was an outstanding monarch butterfly migration. As I walked in midafternoon along Sapsucker Ridge I could see hundreds migrating overhead. One black cherry tree at the top of the ridge was filled with dozens of fluttering and resting monarchs. It resembled the photographs I had seen of their wintering grounds in the mountains of Mexico, where all the trees are plastered with monarchs. The monarchs in the single cherry tree swayed in the wind and opened and closed their brilliant orange wings that glowed in the sunlight.

At the Far Field the goldenrod and asters were covered with monarch butterflies. I stood mesmerized for many minutes in the midst of them as they fluttered down around me—surrounded by a field of monarchs lit like stained glass windows by the clear autumn light.

SEPTEMBER 12. Late summer is certainly the best of times—gleaming with goldenrod, brilliant blue skies, and masses of white snakeroot. Biting insects are almost gone so it's back to basking in the sun and shade in comfort. Cicadas and crickets call by day; katydids by night.

As I walked across First Field in midmorning, a northern harrier sailed up from the grasses in front of me, continuing to dive and hunt for food as I watched. Then slowly it soared higher and higher and was joined by two turkey vultures in a short aerial ballet of infinite grace before a red-tailed hawk appeared from the ridge top. Finally all four headed south along Sapsucker Ridge, a foretaste of the autumnal raptor migration.

I climbed up David's new Big Tree Trail to the top of Sapsucker Ridge. There I was rewarded with a view of a fluffy, white-tailed gray squirrel that skulked down a nearby tree and then dashed off into the forest, its white tail as easy to follow as a beacon light.

I sat at the base of a tree and was so disturbed by the highway noise that I moved on in disgust, wondering why I even bothered to walk along Sapsucker Ridge now that we have the newly designated Interstate 99 roaring below. In addition, the old logging trail leads through a wall of black locust and striped maple saplings that block out any view of the woods beyond.

Then, as I neared the old haul road, a black bear crossed it without seeing me. I remained rooted to the spot as first one cub, then a second one emerged from the underbrush less than ten feet away and ambled after their mother. All disappeared quietly into the thick underbrush without seeing me. For me, it was a dream come true. At last I had seen a mother bear with cubs on the mountain.

I sat down no more than forty feet away from where they had gone and tried to peer through the cover where I could hear the snap of branches. Evidently, the sow was pulling down something for her cubs to eat. I waited several minutes, but heard no further movements, so I cautiously approached the area. She had completely broken down a Hercules' club tree and brought the clusters of still green berries to the ground. However, she must have caught my scent because they were gone as silently as they had first appeared to me. A fresh large plop of bear scat, black and filled with wild black cherry pits, adorned the small clearing.

Even though aesthetically I still find the clear-cut difficult to appreciate, the bears have no such feelings. To them it is a good place to eat and hide from humans.

SEPTEMBER 13. On an early morning walk I found a fungus hanging from a dead log that looked like white stalactites in a cave. According to Louis C. C. Krieger's *The Mushroom Handbook,* its popular name is bear's head Hydnum (*Hydnum caput-ursi*), which is found most often on the dead wood of deciduous trees.

I pished in a male hooded warbler on the Far Field Road. There were lots of snorting deer and calling chipmunks in the woods. A chipmunk with a stubby tail foraged nearby as I sat under the cherry tree in the Far Field woods. As I watched, it popped into a hole three feet from where I was sitting. Last year I watched a chipmunk use this same hole but it didn't have a stubby tail. Could it have lost a part of its tail while escaping a predator, or is this a different chipmunk? Always more questions than answers in the natural world.

I walked down our mountain road and found four more pinesaps growing on the road bank across from the old corral. The count is now up to nineteen.

At 6:10 P.M. a sun dog formed on the clouds near the western horizon. This partial halo is said to be "parhelia" with the sun and is sometimes referred to as a mock sun. It is caused by light refracting through water droplets and ice crystals in the atmosphere. According to the charming book *It's Raining Frogs and Fishes* by Jerry Dennis, this phenomenon is most common when the sun is low in the sky and shining through light cirrus clouds.

SEPTEMBER 14. The cut-leaved grape-fern that David found two years ago growing at the entrance to Guesthouse Trail has sent up its erect spore case. Also known as dissected or ternate grape-fern (*Botrychium dissectum*), it has recently been split by taxonomists. The more unusual, *f. dissectum,* is very finely cut with a lacy appearance. The more common form is *f. obliquum,* which is what we have. Unlike most ferns, which produce spores in June or early July, it sends up its distinctive sporophyll (fertile seed case) in late August on the same stalk as its leaf but an inch or two above it. At the same time it puts out sterile leaves that last through the winter and spring, although they turn bronze after the first frost. Six inches away from the fertile plant, I found a much smaller sterile leaf growing, so it too, like the nodding ladies' tresses, is spreading. Then, along the Far Field Road, I discovered four more sterile leaves. It's amazing how many times we find a new plant in one place and then seem to see it everywhere after that. Has finding the one plant opened our eyes to the presence of others or have they coincidentally appeared in concert with the other?

SEPTEMBER 15. This cool, clear morning was a perfect day to hunt for salamanders in the hollow, and I was finally accompanied by a friend, Stan, and his six-year-old daughter, Helena, who were swift in capturing and accurate in identifying the elusive creatures.

We met at the bottom of the mountain. Salamanders, it turned out, are Helena's favorite herps—naturalists' nickname for reptiles and amphibians. She especially enjoys holding them. At six, she possesses more knowledge of and affinity for salamanders than most adults will ever have. Dressed in camouflage pants and hat, a purple fleece jacket, and hip boots, the brown-haired, brown-eyed girl was not the picture of six-year-old chic, but she was appropriately dressed for wading in our stream. And wade she did, thoroughly enjoying her search for creatures living in and beside the water.

Like all children who have been encouraged to enjoy the outdoors, she has endless curiosity about the natural world. Already she can identify many of the plants and wild creatures she sees in the woods, including the jewelweed that lines our stream bank at the bottom of the hollow.

It was there that we found our first two northern dusky salamanders (*Desmognathus fuscus fuscus*). A member of the genus *Desmognathus,* a genus that Roger Conant and Joseph T. Collins describe in their excellent field guide, *Reptiles and Amphibians Eastern/Central North America,* as more difficult to identify than fall warblers, northern duskies are almost as changeable as chameleons. "Added to changes in coloration and pattern associated with age and size are bewildering individual variations plus differences between one local population and the next," Conant and Collins write (259). Altogether we found nine—under rocks in our stream, crawling beside the stream, under a rock in a wet ravine, and under rocks on the road bank.

"It's amazing how on just one stream you find such color variations," Stan commented, which aptly summed up the bewildering color schemes we discovered including one with a light beige back. That one also shed its tail in an effort to escape, an antipredator behavior called "autonomy." The tail kept wriggling, but we were not fooled. We knew that the salamander would quickly grow a new tail, so we grabbed for the salamander itself despite the fascination of the wriggling tail.

We found only two other salamander species today. One was a northern spring salamander (*Gyrinophilus porphyriticus porphyriticus*) which Stan scooped out of the stream, a mottled, salmon-colored salamander that haunts cool springs and mountain streams. Then, first I and then Stan found a slimy salamander under road bank rocks.

Our incidental discoveries were two crayfishes and a coiled garter snake beneath a rock. The latter was too cold to move, but the crayfishes were lively enough.

We spent only three hours searching and went only a quarter of the way up the stream. Nevertheless, it seemed as if the salamander population is as plentiful and as lively as when my sons were young and searched the hollow for salamanders.

SEPTEMBER 16. It was fifty-two degrees and heavily overcast this morning, but when I set out on my walk there was a warbler migration in the yard. I could see only the black-throated greens clearly, but there were many other species as well.

A single pinesap grew in the moss at the edge of Guesthouse Trail, a bit further up the trail from where those first pinesaps grew in profusion back in 1984 and 1985, giving me a grand total of twenty for the year.

Eastern towhees called incessantly at the Far Field as I searched for the nodding ladies' tresses. Instead of the original sixteen, I found only five blossoms. Two blossoms had been clipped off and lay dying. Many more naked stems had been stripped of their blossoms. Since this is a favorite deer grazing spot, I assumed that the culprits were deer. It looks as if we must fence this spot to save the nodding ladies' tresses just as we did to save the round-leaved orchid from the "hoofed locusts," as some plant enthusiasts call Pennsylvania's overabundant white-tailed deer.

The stub-tailed chipmunk foraged in the forest near my favorite black cherry tree. Then, as I sat quietly, two fawns, one of which was still spotted, grazed to within twenty feet of where I was sitting before one looked up, stamped its front feet, and ran off. The second did the same, just as the first rain started to fall.

No one can deny the infinite grace and beauty of deer, both adults and young, and yet the destruction they are causing to our flora is stupendous in some areas. Finding a balance between deer and plants is still a dilemma for wildlife managers. Botanists, on the other hand, know that ten deer per square mile is best for the health of the forest. Such a statistic is anathema to many hunters who prefer to find a deer behind every tree. So the Pennsylvania Game Commission is trying to compromise at twenty deer per square mile, a goal that they are far from reaching in some areas. To most people, hunters and nonhunters alike, seeing a deer in the forest is far more exciting than a wildflower. And so the debate continues.

SEPTEMBER 17. Today I walked up the hollow road to identify late-blooming wildflowers. What a bonanza I found. By looking closely at the myriad of plants, I added several new wildflowers to our mountain list by the end of the day.

First, at the bottom of the mountain near our gate I found panicled asters, small white asters, and calico or starved asters, all of which are closely related species. A few feet further up the road I stopped to admire a lilac-colored aster with distinctive leaves—the wavy-leaved aster. The weed at the bottom of the mountain was spotted knapweed. I also found great variation in blue-stemmed goldenrod, the most common of the goldenrod species growing in the woods.

Old familiar plants included a Jerusalem artichoke near the gate, white wood asters, beechdrops on the road bank, Indian tobacco (the most common of the lobelias), and several magnificent stands of turtlehead. One particularly nice turtlehead plant had a large-winged, orange insect sitting on a clump of the white, purple-tipped flowers.

I also admired the seeds of spring wildflowers—the large, oval-shaped, red-orange seeds of Solomon's plume and, across the stream, the clustered red seeds of jack-in-the-pulpit gleaming amid the understory of green ferns like Christmas jewels. Jewelweeds—both orange and yellow—were also in seed, and I enjoyed myself popping them, ignoring the exhortation in their other common name, "touch-me-not."

Halfway up the hollow road I found a large-leaved aster. Next to it was another white aster that was not in my field guide. It had linear-shaped leaves, small flowers with pale yellow centers radiating outward, yellow-tipped stamens, and reflexed white petals. Asters, like goldenrod, are American natives and frequently interbreed, so it may have been some sort of hybrid.

To end my walk, I stopped in the lower part of First Field to admire a mass of purple-stemmed asters, one of which had a tiger swallowtail butterfly feeding on it.

SEPTEMBER 18. Heavy autumnlike wind clouds provided plenty of soaring pleasure for turkey vultures who glided over First Field early this afternoon when I set out on my walk. Already the black gum trees have begun to turn; many are scarlet from top to bottom as summer segues into autumn.

I walked up Guesthouse Trail, then went left on Laurel Ridge Trail to Lady Slipper Trail. There I turned left again and followed the Pit Mound Trail down to the Black Gum Trail. I pished up a couple of black-capped chickadees on Lady Slipper Trail, but except for katydids and chipmunks, the woods were quiet.

Later in the afternoon, lying at the top of First Field, I watched raptors skimming past high and fast and monarch butterflies fluttering by also high in the sky. Now that autumn is almost here, it's time to spend hours wrapped in a world of wind and clouds and sunlight, watching raptors migrating south, and serenaded still by a deafening chorus of katydids, a chorus that will diminish as temperatures drop and the raptor migration increases. As I descended First Field, I noticed another sun dog developing in the western sky.

Still loathe to give up a lovely summer day, I walked down the road to meet Bruce and flushed a Swainson's thrush so that it flew up out of the underbrush and landed on a log where I could examine its buffy eye ring, its dull brown back and sides, its lightly spotted breast, and grayish belly. It too is heading south.

SEPTEMBER 19. A heavy dew on First Field shimmered in the sunlight. On the trail across the field, I found a pretty little eastern milk snake so small that it probably recently hatched since this is the time of year for them to do so.

Along the Greenbrier Trail, as I walked in Margaret's Woods, a fat, silver animal waddled toward me—a porcupine with all its quills erect, backlit by the glowing sunshine. Its head was down as it watched where it was going so I quietly stepped off the trail and sat on a log to watch. When it came to within forty-eight feet of me, it stopped, looked up, sniffed the air, and then slowly turned off the trail away from me, still at its same measured pace.

Blue jays continually called as I walked along. The source of their alarm—a mature red-tailed hawk—took off, circling higher and higher as it screamed back at the jays. A gray squirrel scolded me while a fox squirrel fled silently into the underbrush. Eastern towhees and American robins also called.

The clear-cut Dogwood Knoll, as usual, was hot and depressing. So was Ten Springs Trail, choked in blackberry canes. It was a relief to drop into the cool, shaded hollow and hear the first chipmunks of the day. I sat beside the stream to eat my midmorning apple, listening to the water rippling over the stones and watching dappled patches of sunlight.

I pished in a male, black-throated blue warbler, who came from across the stream and landed directly overhead. Black-throated blue warblers, I have recently discovered, respond as well as chickadees to pishing. I also saw an immature rose-breasted grosbeak and heard hordes of blue jays yelling as they harvested acorns from the trees.

Sitting on the veranda in midafternoon admiring the deep blue sky and bands of glittering goldenrod in First Field, in between reading and note taking, I glanced up to see a northern harrier banking low over the field. Back and forth it went and then circled higher and higher as I watched, the white searchlight above its tail an easy identifying mark. As it spiraled above the treetops, it moved slowly down Sapsucker Ridge and then circled into the infinite blue on its way across to Laurel Ridge where it finally disappeared from sight.

To finish the day, Bruce and I went walking at 8:30 P.M. under the light of a full moon. First Field was white with moonlight, and we walked to the top for a moonlit view. The sky was absolutely clear, the stars bright, and the earth drenched with pale light.

Then we headed along the Laurel Ridge Trail, our eyes nearly blinded by the moonlight as we walked into the moon for a short time. It cast white patches through the leaf cover or caught the shine of laurel leaves. Once a deer snorted and ran. Then we heard foxes barking, and finally a low growl off in the underbrush. We paused and waited but heard no more until Bruce tossed a heavy branch toward the direction of the growl and an animal thumped off—probably a bear. We hated to give up the magic of the harvest moon night and return to reality, but after more than an hour we reluctantly went inside to showers and bed.

SEPTEMBER 20. I waited until midmorning to walk the Black Gum Trail. Acorns rained from trees that were motionless in the still air. Blue jays were noisy as usual. So were the chipmunks and squirrels, all, no doubt, excited by the abundant acorn crop. Grouse drummed in the distance and deer dashed through the undergrowth. While last night's walk was a black and white extravaganza, this morning's was one in living color as patches of black gum trees lit up the forest with shades of orange, yellow, pink, red, and purple.

Eventually the warm sun and a soft bed of moss enticed me to lie down for a brief rest. I had no sooner settled myself than I heard an animal moving toward me that I thought was a squirrel. Seconds later, what looked like an attractive gray and brown dog quietly materialized from the underbrush fifteen feet away. This creature had a longer, narrower nose than a dog, and it held its black-tipped tail downward.

After years of finding only circumstantial evidence, such as tracks and scat, I was finally face to face with an eastern coyote.

For several seconds, we stared at each other. Then the coyote turned away and bounded slowly down the trail, pausing several times but never looking back at me.

The coyote's scientific name is *Canis latrans,* meaning "barking dog." Its common name is a derivative of the Aztec god Coyotlinauatl, whose worshippers dressed in coyote skins. Native North Americans in the desert southwest called the coyote "God's Dog" and believed the animal was sent down to Earth to observe humans and then report on their behavior to the deity.

The Crow Indians consider the coyote to be First Worker, the creator of Earth and all living creatures. As founder of human customs, Coyote is a fallible but clever creature, capable of duplicity and of being duped.

Until this century the coyote was a western species respected by Native Americans who rarely killed the animal. As European settlers moved west with their cattle and sheep, wiping out the large predators, only the coyote remained a threat to their domestic animals. Unlike their predator counterparts—grizzly bears, wolves, and mountain lions—the greater the number of coyotes killed, the more replacement pups the remaining coyotes produced. In fact, the adaptive coyote has tripled its range since pre-European settlement times, moving north as far as Alaska, south to Costa Rica in Central America, and even into eastern North America from Newfoundland south to Florida, filling a niche vacated when most large predators were extirpated.

On their move east from Minnesota above Lake Superior and across Wisconsin, coyotes eventually reached northern Michigan and southern Ontario. There they probably mated with timber wolves, tentatively explaining why the eastern coyote is larger than its western counterpart. Researchers who study eastern coyote pups find that they are more sociable than western coyote pups—more playful, less aggressive, and less dominant in their behavior—all wolflike traits.

Recent DNA studies of the eastern coyote determined it is a new animal, but these studies could not find a genetic marker that distinguished coyotes from wolves or dogs. As Ray Coppinger, professor of biology at Hampshire College in Amherst, Massachusetts, explains, "There is more difference between different breeds of dogs than between dogs and wolves" (Smith, 27).

Coyotes eat primarily wild and not domestic animals. Here in Pennsylvania, woodchuck tops the coyote's list of preferred prey, followed by smaller members of the rodent family. In summer and fall, they eat mostly fruit. Stray dogs and cats are taken, along with skunks, raccoons, and opossums. Coyotes occasionally kill white-tailed deer, chiefly the sick, injured, or very young, but most deer is consumed as carrion.

Eastern coyotes weigh from thirty-five to sixty pounds and, like wolves, often run in small packs. In each pack, an alpha male and female pair do all the breeding in their five- to twenty-five-square-mile home range. They breed in late January through mid-February, and five to seven pups are born from mid-April to mid-May in an underground den.

At first the male is the chief hunter, supplying the nursing female with food. Although the pups are born blind and helpless, their eyes open when they are just two weeks old and they venture out of the den a week later. At that point the mother joins the father in hunting food that is later regurgitated, partly digested, for the pups. Young are weaned at eight to nine weeks of age when the family abandons the den. Their instruction in hunting begins in late August, with parents and pups moving over a thirty-square-mile area. The family group disbands in late summer or early autumn. Obviously I had seen a youngster, as a young coyote doesn't reach full size until it is a year old, and, unlike the western coyote, rarely breeds until its second year.

To have finally seen a coyote in the woods was the icing on the cake for what has been an exciting summer of wildlife encounters.

SEPTEMBER 21. Summer is going out in a blaze of glory. The eastern phoebe regained his voice this morning after becoming silent in late June. The phoebe was followed by an eastern bluebird song.

Seventeen college students from the University Scholars Program at Penn State University's Altoona campus, accompanied by their advisor, came to hike our property with me this afternoon. Like a teacher, I properly stopped and lectured at appropriate points on such issues as forestry practices, the history of our property, its flora and fauna, and they, like the good students they were, stopped and respectfully listened to what I was saying, but they had no questions of their own. I felt as if I were trying to fill empty vessels. Some faces did react; some students were interested, and I moved them up the hollow road, around the mountaintop trails, and down Black Gum and Rhododendron trails, about four and a half miles, in four hours, with a long stop on the veranda to eat lunch.

Probably the highlight of the walk was seeing a highly ornamental eastern box turtle on Sapsucker Ridge Trail. Many had never seen one before! David, who walked in the back, heard two young female students with New York City accents say, "I have never walked so far in my life." Several of the young women, including one majoring in marine science, kept up with me on the Black Gum Trail and asked if bears were dangerous or if I feared other wild creatures in the woods. I told them there was nothing to fear but other humans, that the eastern forests had no really threatening creatures, and that I felt immensely safe here.

"What a relief; how refreshing," the aspiring marine scientist commented, and I felt as if I had become a role model for these young females, all of whom told me that watching televised nature specials had made them believe that everything outside was dangerous. If nothing else, I hope their visit gave them a sense of ease in nature and interest in learning more, at least enough to champion the natural world when it is threatened by development and profit-obsessed humans.

Once again Bruce and I took a moonlit walk. This time we went up First Field Trail and back along the Short Circuit Trail. The moon hadn't risen high enough to shine clearly on that trail. Only occasional small patches were lit. Since it is a rougher trail we had to pick our way along more slowly. Still, the woods were much warmer than the field at that time of night. It was the field, however, bathed in moon and star light, that shimmered with unearthly beauty.

SEPTEMBER 22. Fifty-eight degrees and raining at dawn. With less than twelve hours to go before fall officially arrives, it began raining at 3:30 A.M. By midmorning it was still heavily overcast, but the rain had stopped for a time. Gusty winds brought down a shower of water and acorns as I walked Laurel Ridge Trail. A pileated woodpecker called loudly several times. Already the black gums were dressed in their autumnal best, setting the mood for the approaching autumnal light and darkness. It was fitting that this wet summer rained itself out and that the cool green woods of summer were giving way to the bright warm colors of early autumn.

Another Appalachian summer has gone almost before it has started. What a summer it has been, full of new discoveries and old verities. Visitors have often filled our home, eager to see our first grandchild, the first on either side of our families and proof that generation will succeed generation. The oldest visitor was my eighty-two-year-old father, our only surviving parent, who was pleased to meet his first great-grandchild.

It takes so many years for each human generation to mature, yet in only one summer many generations of insects mature and one or more generations of birds and mammals. Each has its own time line and for those whose lives are short, in human terms, this may have been the only summer they will ever know.

This has been my fifty-sixth summer on earth and I keenly feel its passing. Every summer has its own special aura, but this one, with its new generation, shall remain a bright memory that I will treasure for the rest of my life.

Postscript

And thus when, hearing her mother's frightened voice, she appeared finally from the dark tangle of trees and shrubs, her face was so radiant that her mother, amazed to see this new joy in her daughter, did not tell her then what she knew she would soon have to say. That those bushes her daughter hid behind can also hide strangers, that for her shadows speak danger, that in such places little girls must be afraid.

—Susan Griffin, *Women and Nature: The Roaring Inside Her*

Several months later, Ronald K. Isenberg, Jr., the male teenager the searchers had been looking for that July night in 1996, was arrested on a theft charge. Only once, to a female aide at a juvenile detention center, has he confessed to the murder of Melody. A Blair County judge decided that his alleged confession was coerced and that rape could not be proved because Melody's body was so badly decomposed. The Pennsylvania Superior Court recently reversed that decision, ruling that the confession of Isenberg was legally valid and that the prosecutors had offered enough evidence to charge him with rape. Isenberg's lawyers are now appealing that decision. But the prosecution, too, is tenacious as the case wends its torturous way through the court system. We can only hope that justice will be done.

No matter what the final decision will be, though, neither

her heartbroken grandmother nor the people of Tyrone will forget what was done to that innocent child. Along Interstate 99, a couple of hundred feet from where her body was found, a memorial was erected shortly after her funeral. Drivers whizzing by see only a large heart, made of small stones, enclosing a stone tombstone. At the top of the heart a large wooden cross has *Melody Curtis* inscribed on its crossbeam and a color photograph of her on the vertical beam. A small cross of white flowers stands at one corner of the heart and another small cross of red flowers on the opposite side. Outside the heart a painted wooden angel stands guard. Rest in peace, Melody.

Marcia Bonta
November 1998

Selected Bibliography
Index

Selected Bibliography

General

Aurora, David. *Mushrooms Demystified: A Comprehensive Guide to the Fleshy Fungi.* Berkeley, Calif.: Ten Speed Press, 1979.

Berry, Thomas. *The Dream of the Earth.* San Francisco: Sierra Club Books, 1988.

Bonta, Mark. *Bioplum: A Biological Inventory of the Bonta Property and Adjacent Parcels, Northern Brush Mountain, Blair County, Pennsylvania.* Plummer's Hollow, Pa.: 1991.

Borland, Hal. *Twelve Moons of the Year.* New York: Alfred A. Knopf, 1979.

Brooks, Maurice. *The Appalachians.* Boston: Houghton Mifflin, 1965.

Bryant, William Cullen. *Poems.* New York: Harper & Brothers, 1843.

Davis, F. W. In Arthur Cleveland Bent, *Life Histories of North American Birds of Prey.* 2 vols. New York: Dover Publications, 1961.

Dennis, Jerry. *It's Raining Frogs and Fishes: Four Seasons of Natural Phenomena and Oddities of the Sky.* New York: Harper Collins, 1992.

Eiseley, Loren. *The Immense Journey.* New York: Random House, 1946.

Jenkins, David T. *Mushrooms: A Separate Kingdom.* Birmingham, Ala.: Oxmoor House, 1979.

Krieger, Louis C. C. *The Mushrooms of North America.* New York: Dutton, 1979.

Linscott, Robert N., ed. *Selected Poems and Letters of Emily Dickinson.* Garden City, N.Y.: Doubleday & Co., 1959.

Miller, Orson K., Jr. *Mushrooms of North America.* New York: Dutton, 1979.

Nabhan, Gary Paul, and Stephen Trimble. *The Geography of Childhood: Why Children Need Wild Places.* Boston: Beacon Press, 1994.

Oliver, Mary. *American Primitive.* Boston: Little, Brown & Co., 1978.

Quammen, David. *Natural Acts: A Sidelong View of Science and Nature.* New York: Lyons and Burford, 1985.

Sims, Grant. "Life in the Slow Lane." *National Wildlife* 31 (Aug./Sept. 1993): 16–23.

Tomlinson, H. M. *The Sea and the Jungle.* Barre, Mass.: The Imprint Society, 1971.

Torrey, Bradford, and Francis H. Allen, eds. *The Journal of Henry D. Thoreau.* 2 vols. New York: Dover Publications, 1962.

Weidensaul, Scott. *Mountains of the Heart: A Natural History of the Appalachians.* Golden, Colo.: Fulcrum, 1994.

Whitman, Walt. *Leaves of Grass.* New York: Dutton, 1947.

Birds

Anonymous. "A Growing Dove Needs Plenty of Fresh Milk." *Audubon* 76 (May 1974): 16–18.

Bent, Arthur Cleveland. *Life Histories of North American Birds of Prey.* 2 vols. New York: Dover Publications, 1961.

———. *Life Histories of North American Cardinals, Grosbeaks, Buntings, Towhees, Finches, Sparrows and Their Allies.* 3 vols. New York: Dover Publications, 1968.

———. *Life Histories of North American Flycatchers, Larks, Swallows, and Their Allies.* New York: Dover Publications, 1963.

———. *Life Histories of North American Gallinaceous Birds.* Washington, D.C.: Smithsonian Institution, 1932.

———. *Life Histories of North American Nuthatches, Wrens, Thrashers, and Their Allies.* New York: Dover Publications, 1964.

———. *Life Histories of North American Woodpeckers.* New York: Dover Publications, 1964.

Brauning, Daniel W., ed. *Atlas of Breeding Birds in Pennsylvania.* Pittsburgh: University of Pittsburgh Press, 1992.

Brown, Leslie, and Dean Amadon. *Eagles, Hawks, and Falcons of the World.* New York: McGraw-Hill, 1968.

Craig, Wallace. "The Expression of Emotion in the Pigeons. II, The Mourning Dove." *The Auk* 28 (Oct. 1911): 398–407.

Gehlbach, Frederick R. "Odd Couples of Suburbia." *Natural History* 95 (June 1986): 56–66.

Heintzelman, Donald S. "Spring and Summer Sparrow Hawk Food Habits." *The Wilson Bulletin* 76 (Dec. 29, 1964): 323–30.

Jackson, Jerome A. "Down the Hatch." *Birder's World* 8 (Dec. 1994): 12–16.

Kilham, Lawrence. *Woodpeckers of Eastern North America.* New York: Dover Publications, 1992.

Nice, Margaret Morse. "A Study of the Nesting of Mourning Doves." *The Auk* 40 (Jan. 1932): 37–58.

Peterson, Roger Tory. *A Field Guide to the Birds of Eastern and Central North America*. Boston: Houghton Mifflin, 1980.

Pravosudor, V. V., and T. C. Gubb Jr. "White-Breasted Nuthatch." *The Birds of North America* no. 54 (1993): 1–14.

Rensel, Jack Arthur. "The Life History, Ecology and Productivity of the Mourning Dove in Central Pennsylvania." Master's thesis, Pennsylvania State University, University Park, 1952.

Skutch, Alexander. *The Minds of Birds*. College Station: Texas A & M University Press, 1996.

Stokes, Donald W. *A Guide to Bird Behavior: Volume I*. Boston: Little, Brown, 1979.

Stokes, Donald W., and Lillian Q. Stokes. *A Guide to Bird Behavior: Volume II*. Boston: Little, Brown, 1983.

———. *A Guide to Bird Behavior: Volume III*. Boston: Little, Brown, 1989.

Terres, John K. *The Audubon Society Encyclopedia of North American Birds*. New York: Alfred A. Knopf, 1982.

Insects and Spiders

Agosta, William. *Bombardier Beetles and Fever Trees: A Close-up Look at Chemical Warfare and Signals in Animals and Plants*. Reading, Mass.: Addison-Wesley Publishing Co., 1996.

Berenbaum, May R. *Bugs in the System: Insects and Their Impact on Human Affairs*. Reading, Mass.: Addison-Wesley Publishing Co., 1995.

Borror, Donald J., and Richard E. White. *A Field Guide to the Insects of America North of Mexico*. Boston: Houghton Mifflin, 1970.

Buchmann, Stephen L., and Gary Paul Nabhan. *The Forgotten Pollinators*. Washington, D.C.: Island Press, 1996.

Covell, Charles V., Jr. *Eastern Moths*. Boston: Houghton Mifflin, 1984.

Evans, David L., and Justin O. Schmidt, ed. *Insect Defenses: Adaptive Mechanisms and Strategies of Prey and Predators*. Albany: State University of New York Press, 1990.

Evans, Howard Ensign. *Life on a Little-Known Planet*. New York: Dutton, 1968.

Henry, Charles S. "Good Vibrations." *Natural History* 95 (Aug. 1986): 47–52.

Hillyard, Paul. *The Book of the Spider: From Arachnophobia to the Love of Spiders*. New York: Random House, 1994.

Holland, W. J. *The Moth Book: A Popular Guide to a Knowledge of the Moths of North America.* New York: Dover Publications, 1968.

Horsfall, William R., Harland W. Fowler Jr., Louis J. Moretti, and Joseph R. Larsen. *Bionomics and Embryology of the Inland Flood-water Mosquito Aedes vexans.* Urbana: University of Illinois Press, 1973.

McMillan, Vicky. "Dragonfly Monopoly." *Natural History* 93 (July 1984): 33–39.

Mitchell, Robert T., and Herbert S. Zim. *Butterflies and Moths: A Guide to the More Common American Species.* New York: Golden Press, 1964.

Nielsen, Lewis T. "Mosquitoes Unlimited." *Natural History* 100 (July 1991): 4–6.

Opler, Paul A., and Vichai Malikul. *Eastern Butterflies.* Boston: Houghton Mifflin, 1992.

Pyle, Robert Michael. *Handbook for Butterfly Watchers.* Boston: Houghton Mifflin, 1984.

Stokes, Donald W. *A Guide to Observing Insect Lives.* Boston: Little, Brown, 1983.

Teale, Edwin Way. *Near Horizons.* New York: Dodd, Mead, 1942.

Worth, C. Brooke. *Of Mosquitoes, Moths and Mice.* New York: W. W. Norton & Co., 1972.

Mammals

Arthur, Stephen M., William B. Krohn, and James R. Gilbert. "Habitat Use and Diet of Fishers." *Journal of Wildlife Management* 53 (fall 1989): 680–88.

Boer, Arnold H. *Ecology and Management of the Eastern Coyote.* Fredericton, New Brunswick: Wildlife Research Unit, University of New Brunswick, 1992.

Fritzell, Erik K., and Kurt J. Haroldson. "Urocyon cinereoargenteus." *Mammalian Species* 189 (Nov. 23, 1982): 1–8.

Gilbert, Bil. "A Groundhog's Day Means More to Us Than It Does to Him." *Smithsonian* 15 (February 1985): 60–69.

———. "Coyotes Adapted to Us, Now We Have to Adapt to Them." *Smithsonian* 21 (March 1991): 69–79.

Hamilton, William J., Jr., and John O. Whitaker Jr. *Mammals of the Eastern United States.* Ithaca: Cornell University Press, 1979.

Hayden, Arnold H. "The Eastern Coyote Revisited." *Pennsylvania Game News* 60 (Dec. 1989): 12–15.

Krohn, William B., and Kenneth D. Elowe. "Do the Pieces Fit?" *Maine Fish and Wildlife* 35 (fall 1993): 6–11.

Merritt, Joseph F. *Guide to the Mammals of Pennsylvania.* Pittsburgh: University of Pittsburgh Press, 1987.

Parker, Gerry. *Eastern Coyote: The Story of Its Success.* Halifax, Nova Scotia: Nimbus Publishing Limited, 1995.

Peterson, Karen E., and Terry L. Yates. "Condylura cristata." *Mammalian Species* 129 (April 15, 1980): 1–4.

Powell, Roger A. *The Fisher: Life History, Ecology and Behavior.* Minneapolis: University of Minnesota Press, 1993.

Rupp, J. Scott. "Return of the Fisher." *Pennsylvania Game News* 66 (Feb. 1995): 4–7.

Ryden, Hope. *God's Dog: A Celebration of the North American Coyote.* New York: Lyons & Burford, 1975.

Smith, Charles W. G. "Yellow Eyes." *Country Journal* 19 (March/April 1992): 26–31.

Wood, John. "What Is a Fisher?" *National Wildlife* 15 (April/May 1977): 18–21.

Yates, Terry L. "The Mole That Keeps Its Nose Clean." *Natural History* 92 (Nov. 1983): 54–61.

Plants

Cobb, Boughton. *A Field Guide to the Ferns.* Boston: Houghton Mifflin, 1956.

Durant, Mary. *Who Named the Daisy? Who Named the Rose? A Roving Dictionary of North American Wildflowers.* New York: Congdon & Weed, 1976.

Gibbons, Euell. *Stalking the Healthful Herbs.* New York: David McKay Co., 1973.

Grimm, William Carey. *The Shrubs of Pennsylvania.* Harrisburg: Stackpole and Heck, 1952.

———. *The Trees of Pennsylvania.* Harrisburg: Stackpole and Heck, 1950.

Hallowell, Anne C., and Barbara G. Hallowell. *Fern Finder: A Guide to Native Ferns of Northeastern and Central North America.* Berkeley, Calif.: Nature Study Guild, 1981.

Harned, Joseph E. *Wild Flowers of the Alleghanies.* Oakland, Md.: Press of the Sincell Printing Company, 1931.

Mickel, John T. *How to Know the Ferns and Fern Allies.* Dubuque, Ia.: William C. Brown Company, 1979.

Morse, Douglass H. "Milkweeds and Their Visitors." *Scientific American* 253 (Sept. 1985): 112–19.

Niles, Grace Greylock. *Bog-Trotting for Orchids.* New York: G. P. Putnam's & Sons, 1904.

Peattie, Donald Culross. *A Natural History of Trees of Eastern and Central North America,* 2d ed. New York: Bonanza Books, 1966.

Peterson, Roger Tory, and Margaret McKenny. *A Field Guide to Wildflowers of Northeastern and Northcentral North America.* Boston: Houghton Mifflin, 1968.

Sanders, Jack. *Hedgemaids and Fairy Candles: The Lives and Lore of North American Wildflowers.* Camden, Me.: Ragged Mountain Press, 1993.

Reptiles and Amphibians

Babcock, Harold L. *Turtles of the Northeastern United States.* New York: Dover Publications, 1971.

Blaustein, Andrew R., and David B. Wake. "The Puzzle of Declining Amphibian Populations." *Scientific American* 272 (April 1995): 52–57.

Conant, Roger, and Joseph T. Collins. *Reptiles and Amphibians of Eastern/Central North America.* Boston: Houghton Mifflin, 1991.

Ernst, Carl H., and Roger W. Barbour. *Turtles of the World.* Washington, D.C.: Smithsonian Institution Press, 1989.

Green, N. Bayard, and Thomas K. Pauley. *Amphibians and Reptiles in West Virginia.* Pittsburgh: University of Pittsburgh Press, 1987.

Shaffer, Larry L. *Pennsylvania Amphibians and Reptiles.* Harrisburg: Pennsylvania Fish Commission, 1991.

Index

208   *Index*

64, 73, 133; departure of 157; and window-washing, 55
Bonta, Mark (author's son), xv, xvi, 8, 25, 64, 69; departure of, 157; observing rough-winged swallows, 74; observing star-nosed mole, 80; and road work, 99; and window-washing, 55
Bonta, Steven (author's son), xv, 68, 85; fishing in Little Juniata River, 151; observing American kestrels, 144
Botrychium dissectum, 184
Bouncing bet, 109
Brooks, Maurice, 91
Bryant, William Cullen, 127
Buchmann, Stephen L., 84
Bucknell University, x, xii
Bunting, indigo, 97
Burroughs, John, 124
Bush-clover, hairy, 159
Butter-and-eggs, 150
Butterfly, life history of, 94–96; wings of, 151, 152
Butterfly, American copper, 73; mating of, 164
Butterfly, Baltimore, 95
Butterfly, black swallowtail, 109
Butterfly, cabbage, 72;72, 110
Butterfly, clouded sulphur, 73
Butterfly, common wood nymph, 73
Butterfly, coral hairstreak, 110
Butterfly, gray hairstreak, 53
Butterfly, great-spangled fritillary, 53, 72; feeding on butterflyweed, 82; feeding on milkweed, 110; food of, 109
Butterfly, meadow fritillary, 110
Butterfly, monarch, 110, 176, 177
Butterfly, northern pearly eye, 73
Butterfly, painted lady, 72–73
Butterfly, pearl crescent, 180
Butterfly, question mark, 53, 172
Butterfly, red-spotted purple, 36, 53
Butterfly, silver-spotted skipper, 73, 109, 110
Butterfly, tawny fritillary, 110
Butterfly, tiger swallowtail, 110
Butterfly, white admiral, 53
Butterflyweed, 82

Canis latrans, 192
Carbon County, xii
Catalpa, 53–54
Catalpa bignoniaceae, 54
Catalpa speciosa, 54
Catbird, gray: fledgling of, 39, 118; nest of, 52, 140; singing of, 56
Caterpillar, tent, 48
Catesby, Mark, 53
Chambersburg, Pa., 75
Chickadee, black-capped, 46, 117
Chipmunk, eastern: foraging of, 51–52, 172–73, 184; mating of, 41; nest building, 29–31
Chrysolina hyperici, 109
Chrysoperla plorabunda, 153
Clavariadelphus ligula, 181
Cohosh, black, 83-85
Collins, Joseph T., 186
Conant, Roger, 186
Condylura cristata, 80
Coppinger, Ray, 193
Cowbird, brown-headed, 15
Coyote, eastern, xvi, 191-94
Craig, Wallace, 121
Crayfish, 151, 186
Creeper, brown, 118
Cricket, snowy tree, 160–62
Crow, American, 39
Curtis, Melody, 65–66, 68, 73, 151, 197–98; burial of, 86–87

Daucus carota, 106
Davis, F. W., 103
Deer, white-tailed, xvi, 101–02, 140–41, 170; and damage to plants, 82, 91, 165, 187–88; drinking habits of, 162; and fawn running, 45; and love of salt, 92–93; nursing young, 35; playing of, 142, 166–67; and tame fawn, 57, 60, 62
Dennestaedtia punctilobula, 89
Dennis, Jerry, 184
Deptford pink, 141
Desmognathus fuscus fuscus, 186
Dianthus armeria, 141
Dicksonia pilosiuscula, 89
Distraction-displaying: Baltimore oriole, 49; golden-winged warbler, 15, 40; hooded warbler, 118;